UNFORGETTABLE MEN
IN
UNFORGETTABLE TIMES

Stories of Honor, Courage, Commitment and Faith from World War II

By the author of
A Higher Honor
&
C-Rations For The Warrior's Heart

UNFORGETTABLE MEN
IN
UNFORGETTABLE TIMES

Stories of Honor, Courage, Commitment
and Faith from World War II

Robert Boardman

Foreword by General Charles C. Krulak, USMC

First printing 1998
Second printing 1999
Third printing 2000
Fourth printing 2002
Fifth printing 2004

Printed in the United States of America

Packaged by Selah Publishing Group, Dillsboro, Indiana. The views expressed or implied in this work do not necessarily reflect those of Selah Publishing. Ultimate design, content, and editorial accuracy of this work is the responsibility of the author.

ISBN 1-58930-001-7
Library of Congress Catalog Card Number: 97-62568

DEDICATION

These are the Unforgettable Men

To the Marines and Navy personnel of all six Marine divisions and air wings of World War II.

To my comrades of the First Marine Division and the Division Association which fosters this ongoing camaraderie from all wars and peacetime. Through it I have met some of the men in these stories. We were in the same areas and battles, but didn't know each other at that time.

To the tankers of the Marine Corps from all wars and peacetime and the Marine Corps Tanker's Association and their outstanding work.

To Ed Hukle. I drove for several excellent tank commanders. One of the finest combat Marines I have ever worked with or for on both Peleliu and Okinawa was Platoon Sgt. Ed Hukle, who was badly wounded and evacuated from Okinawa on 11 May 1945. He and I were like hand-in-glove as we operated in battle.

To the officers and men of C Company First Tank Battalion, First Marine Division with whom I served. I am still in touch with the following, several to whom I owe my life:

JOE ALVAREZ

CHARLEY ANDERSON

JERRY ATKINSON

NICK BACKOVICH

D. I . BAHDE*

VERLE BUZZ BARWICK*

ED HUTCHINSON

WALT JAIN

PHIL MALLERY

WALTER MUMU MOORE

JOHN MOORE

Walter Olie Olson
Louie Printz
Cornelius Bud Brenkert*
Glen Old Man Christensen*
Bill Dunn*
W. Orville Finley*
Bill Henahan
Roy Herschberger
Ed Hukle

Ed Hutchinson
Red Saunders
Les Seaberg
Don Seidler
Don Thompson
Wendell Wagner
Irv Wickert
Milton Pappy Gore (B Co.)
Don Richter (Amtracs)

* deceased

To all Marines, Corpsmen, and attached Navy personnel, known and unknown, who sacrificed their lives for freedom, honor, and justice in the Pacific.

CONTENTS

FOREWORD

During World War II, our nation faced one of the greatest challenges in our history. The Marines who fought so bravely against the forces of tyranny in that immense and consuming conflict are forever remembered by us. Their courage and determination are part of our storied legacy. From this legacy we draw lessons, insights, and inspiration.

The pages that follow contain chapters about unforgettable men who demonstrated honor, courage, and commitment in their personal character. Each of these men, embroiled in the cauldron of battle or experiencing the sometimes lingering effects of war in their lives, have provided us with an example that underscores the importance of these values as bedrocks of strength in our lives.

General Charles C. Krulak

Warfare is much more than a test of skill, determination, and military prowess. It is a great crucible, a crucible in which men and unthinkable hardships are meshed together as if by an alchemist of old, the two elements having once been combined, never to be exactly the same again. The events that bring the hardships are shaped by the men present there, and the results become history. The man, however, who endures the challenges of battle goes on with his life. Ironically, how he is able to continue is directly related to how he prepared himself before his wartime experiences—not just in body and mind—but most importantly in spirit.

Preparation of the spirit is a two-part process. Each part is separate yet inextricably linked to the other. First, a man must decide on what traits he will include in his character. Will he be a man to be trusted, one willing to sacrifice for his fellow man, and one who can be counted upon when the chips are down? In the Marine Corps we know these desired characteristics as our core values: honor, courage, and commitment. These are the core values of both our beloved institution and of every man and woman who has earned the right to wear our cherished eagle, globe, and anchor. They provide a great source of strength for all Marines. They are the fundamental building blocks of our character.

The second part of the preparation of our spirit is the development of our faith. In the Holy Scriptures we are told to "Put on the whole armour of God, that you may be able to stand against the wiles of the devil. For we wrestle not against flesh and blood, but against principalities, against powers, against the rulers of the darkness of this world, against spiritual wickedness in high places. Wherefore take unto you the whole armour of God, that you may be able to withstand in the evil day, and having done all, to stand" (Ephesians 6:11–13).

The vignettes in this book are about unforgettable men in unforgettable times. These men should not be forgotten, because each was special. They, after having done all, stand. And they stand holding forth a lantern that can illuminate the path to our own spiritual development. I recommend this fine work to all who seek to strengthen their character and develop their spirit. Look for the light.

Semper Fidelis.

CHARLES C. KRULAK,
GENERAL
US Marine Corps

INTRODUCTION

More than fifty years have passed since the last shot was fired in that great struggle between the forces of the Imperial Japanese Empire and those of the United States and its allies.

While time has softened much of the harshness growing out of that fierce and bloody conflict, there are fortunately survivors of that struggle yet alive to chronicle, for the sake of posterity, certain events that took place. The author of this book is eminently qualified among those still capable of reducing such historical matters to writing. Some he experienced firsthand, and other knowledge he has obtained directly from sources reliable beyond doubt.

Robert Boardman, a native of Oregon, now residing in Seattle, enlisted in the Marine Corps in 1942 as a teenager. He took boot training at Recruit Depot San Diego and a short time later, in the Seventeenth Replacement Battalion, sailed for Australia, where he joined the First Marine Division. The division had just concluded its participation in the Guadalcanal Campaign, the first land offensive against the Japanese in the Pacific.

Bob was assigned to C Company, First Tank Battalion, and served that unit almost to the end of the war. He took part in each campaign in which the First Marine Division was a participant: Cape Gloucester, New Britain; Peleliu, where he was first wounded; and Okinawa, where on 17 June 1945, just south of Kunishi Ridge, his young life was nearly ended. Kunishi was the last great organized bastion of the enemy's defense on Okinawa.

Many of Bob's writings have attracted notice, particularly among WWII Marines and especially among veterans of the First Marine Division. Bob is a life member of the First Marine Division Association and presently serves as unit director, representing the tankers. He does chaplain's work for the association when called upon by the chaplain, and officially he is the chaplain of the Marine Corps Tanker's Association.

The manner in which Bob holds his reader's attention is fascinating. He has gone to great effort to collect numerous interesting observations of Marines at war in the Pacific Theater. Into each story or anecdote he always reveals his deep love and admiration for the works of the Creator, our Lord and Savior, in the person of Jesus Christ.

The primary purpose of the book is to accurately set forth some very important facets of the war in the Pacific. Bob's writings contain a fine anecdotal collection, which include deeds of heroism, perilous struggles, brilliant exploits, and other daring incidents of the war. Each chapter reflects the central theme throughout the book of the necessity of combat Marines making that special commitment, not only to their buddies, their Corps, and their country, but also above all, to God.

I am honored and humbled to have been asked by Bob to write this introduction. My friend, Walter Moore, Col. (Ret.) USMC, except for his current illness, would have been able to write a more meaningful commentary. He and the author served together for many months as members of the First Tank Battalion and for all of the years since then have been very close friends. I only came to know Bob in 1993 at the First Marine Division Association reunion in Houston, since which we have become fast friends. In any event, it is with pleasure that I acknowledge on Bob's behalf the courtesies extended unto him by the brave and chivalrous men and officers whose names are mentioned in these pages and who are yet alive.

Finally, I am convinced that *Unforgettable Men in Unforgettable Times* will be read with great pride by all red-blooded Americans, with the utmost admiration in mind for those officers and men of the United States Marine Corps who met face to face and ultimately overcame a powerful and ruthless enemy.

May it be read, not only by members of the Corps—past, present, and future—but also by every American with the welfare of his country and the beneficence of God above foremost in mind.

W. HARVEY BROCKINGTON
World War II Marine
Charleston, South Carolina

Author's Introduction
Marked for Life

Most of us who enlisted in the Corps in World War II were teenagers. We wanted to be in on the excitement and adventure. The great majority of us had never even seen a dead man. Very few of us had attended a funeral. Death was so far off, so mysterious, vague, and impersonal.

Yet here we were rushing off to become intimately involved with the Grim Reaper—to kill or be killed. Boys became men overnight. This war would cost the entire world "approximately 40,000,000 to 50,000,000, making it the bloodiest conflict as well as the largest war in history," according to the *Encyclopedia Britannica.*

The trauma of World War II during my four-year experience (December 1942–February 1947) marked me for life, as it did so many others of that era. Through my twenty-six months in the Pacific Theater, my outfit, the First Marine Division, engaged a relentless enemy three times; in the deep, unyielding rain forests of Cape Gloucester, New Britain; on the narrow coral and jungle confines of Peleliu; and in the terraced rice fields and rugged, limestone escarpments of semitropical Okinawa.

Prior to my joining the First as a replacement in Australia, they had met and defeated our adversary the Japanese on Guadalcanal, the first American land offensive in the Pacific. For three of these four battles—Guadalcanal, Peleliu, and Okinawa—the First Marine Division was decorated with the presidential unit citation.

Looking back at that short four-year span of my life, I see four main areas in which I was marked for a lifetime.

The *first mark* on my life was made by serving with unforgettable men from all parts of the country. Talk about a broadening experience for all of us—most from small towns and rural areas—this was it! This camaraderie that began fifty-six years ago continues in a very strong manner with certain buddies until today.

My wife, Jean, and I spent thirty-six years of our lives overseas, most of it among the former enemy in Japan. So there were great gaps in contact with these fellow Marines, but it seems to have made little difference. Over time the bond grows stronger and sturdier.

Through training for war and personal battlefield experience with these unforgettable men, I try to show in this book how honor, sacrifice, commitment, courage, and faith overcome fear, personal struggle, and a determined enemy. These chivalrous elements make both men and heroes out of greenhorn youth.

In World War II civilian reserves joined with career professional Marines to produce, in the words of George McMillan, author of *The Old Breed*, "a rare kind of courage, an almost exotic aggressiveness," that eventually helped bring victory and peace to a war-torn and weary world.

The amazing thing about this kind of camaraderie is that it keeps on extending today to men I never knew in World War II and other wars. Knowing what they went through for their country, their God, and fellow warriors, brings a unique bonding. Jean and I have furthered and broadened these relationships by attending reunions and functions of the First Marine Division Association and the Marine Corps Tankers Association, of which it is my honor to serve as chaplain.

The *second indelible mark* was made physically, upon my body. I speak of these wounds not as though they are any more serious than those inflicted by the enemy upon any other servicemen. And certainly not to draw undue attention to them or to feel sorry for myself. However, almost every day of my life I'm called upon to give some kind of explanation for them.

On Peleliu (pel-lel-loo) I was wounded slightly and then on Okinawa received near fatal marks that I thought at the time were taking me on to what the Old Testament prophet Job called "the journey of no return." As a sniper's bullet pierced Jerry Atkinson's neck and then my throat and hand—it is from today's perspective—as if my neck was pierced by Providence. My larynx was destroyed, so now I only speak with a husky whisper.

We often cannot determine the long-range purpose when something first takes place, but we must wait and exercise trust. The detailed story of this wounding is in the chapter "Unforgettable Men in Unforgettable Times" and "The Father's Day Massacre, June 17, 1945."

The *third indelible mark* took place in Australia, toward the beginning of that four-year period. It affected my life more profoundly than the sniper's bullet on Okinawa. I moved from being a dog-tag Christian to becoming a true believer and follower of the Living God. When I entered the Corps, our dog tags were stamped with a *C* for Catholic, a *P* for Protestant or *H* for the Hebrew faith. If you were an atheist or agnostic, you drew a blank on your dog tag. Good luck! I was a *P* simply because I wasn't a *C* or an *H*!

Beginning in Australia, I read a New Testament for three months and consequently said goodbye to dog-tag Christianity. See the chapter "I Fought the Battle of Ballarat, and Lost."

The *fourth unerasable mark* upon my life was my desire to be a lifelong witness for God. This commitment began in the rain forests of Cape Gloucester, after we had secured that area of New Britain. Through still a teenager, I wondered if I could capably serve God because of my limited life experience and training. But I gained peace through reading the Scriptures, and this service has continued for the past sixty years of my life. Marked for life in four short, exciting, unforgettable years in the Corps!

My generation is rapidly passing from the scene. Thousands of World War II veterans die monthly. I read recently that the Department of Veterans Affairs makes this prediction: "Deaths among the GI generation, now in their 70s, are likely to peak in 2008, when 620,000 veteran deaths are projected."

This means an average of 52,000 deaths a month by the year 2008. We each have an appointed length of time upon earth, and then we will be summoned and will take the journey of no return. "Taps" will then be played. We have an outstanding story still to be told. We must not cease from telling the following generations what we've seen and heard.

In World War I, my father served in France with the YMCA and my mother was a Red Cross worker in England. They were married at the time. I recently discovered a yellowed clipping from the Burlington, Iowa, *Hawk-Eye* newspaper, 8 July 1919:

> Mrs. Ada Boardman . . . was in a group of eight American women honored in London by being made "Life Associate Members" of the United States Marine Corps and decorated with gold and silver brooches in recognition of the work done in London Red Cross canteens for the Marines.

Perhaps this was prophetic for my life.

In *Unforgettable Men in Unforgettable Times* I did not mean to neglect other equally valiant Marine divisions and units. I simply did not have the space. Comrades from other outfits, air wings, and other branches of the armed forces are equally responsible for the hard-won victory in the Pacific. My respect and that of all Americans for these fellow warriors has no bounds of gratitude for the indescribable price they also paid.

I pray and believe that this book will deeply touch countless veterans and active-service personnel. As men, women, and young people from all walks of life read these accounts of the men of World War II who looked to God in times of mortal danger, stress, and death, may they be profoundly challenged.

These are deep lessons that all men and women can value for their own lives and for passing on to their children and peers. Personal honor, courage, faith, and commitment in both war and peacetime are vital for the survival of our great nation.

Bob Boardman

I. THE PRICE
OF WAR

ONE

UNFORGETTABLE MEN IN UNFORGETTABLE TIMES
Where the Bullet with My Name on it Found Me

Let the world count the crosses. Let them count them over and over. Let us do away with names, with ranks and rates and unit designations, here. Do away with the terms—regulars, reserve, veteran, boot, old-timers, replacement. They are empty, categorizing words which belong only in the adjutant's dull vocabulary. Here lie only, only Marines.
>—*Maj. Gen. Graves B. Erskine, 14 March 1945.*
>*At the dedication of the Third Marine Division*
>*Cemetery on Iwo Jima*

Except for one shrapnel injury, I had made it safely through three US Marine Corps World War II amphibious landings: Cape Gloucester, Peleliu, and Okinawa. But just four days before the end of combat in Okinawa, I was shot by a Japanese sniper.

Okinawa, the final battle of World War II lasted eighty-one days. The cost for the United States was over 12,500 killed and 36,300 wounded. The Japanese suffered over 131,000 military killed. June 17 was the seventy-eighth day of fighting for this island. Naturally, we didn't know it at the time, but there were just four days to go and we would be out of harm's way and hopefully would be able to go home.

I was in C Company, First Tank Battalion, First Marine Division. Walter "MuMu" Moore was our executive officer. We were attached to and serving with the Seventh Marine Infantry Regiment. At this late stage of the intense battle our company had only

21

a handful of effective tanks left out of fifteen. Soon there would be two less. Today, among the men mentioned in this particular C Company action, there are several chest's full of Purple Hearts, Silver Stars, one Navy Cross, presidential unit citations, and campaign ribbons from battles throughout the Pacific.

How Spilled Coffee Saved a Man's Life

"Wild" Bill Henahan, a skinny guy from Detroit, Michigan, was the crack gunner in Lt. Jerry Atkinson's tank. I was the driver. After a hard day of combat on June 16, Henahan and some other Marines were brewing coffee over a makeshift fire behind the front lines. The scalding liquid accidentally tipped over, severely burning Bill's arm, preventing him from being our gunner the next fateful day. Bill had been in C Company for over two years, and we would miss his expertise. Robert Bennett, from Oklahoma, relatively new to the outfit, "volunteered" to take Henahan's place. Bennett had less than a day to live.

The next morning, June Seventeenth, just over Kunishi Ridge, I maneuvered our tank to face one of the last ridges of resistance on the island. It would not be easy. The Japanese were waiting for us with 47mm and 76mm antitank guns. Within moments, armor-piercing shells hit and disabled our two assault tanks.

Deadly shellfire penetrated the tank I was driving, hitting just behind where I was sitting. One clipped my seat back. Robert Bennett, the gunner taking Bill Henahan's place, was killed instantly by an enemy shell or a ricocheting piece of steel. The same deadly shard gave Lieutenant Atkinson, standing behind Bennett, his first wound of the many he would receive that day. Because Henahan was scalded the evening before, he lived. His substitute, Bennett, never had a fighting chance and never knew what hit him. Any man who has been in combat asks the question, "Why did God allow so-and-so to die, and why did He spare me?" When a bullet or a shell fragment cuts down the man next to you or takes your best buddy, it leaves you pondering the riddle the rest of your life.

Jerry "The Sieve" Atkinson

Lt. Fitzgerald "Jerry" Atkinson out of Nashville, Tennessee came to C Company from officer's training as a young, brash, green second lieutenant. He needed lots of help in learning how to lead troops and we gave it to him. Many of us in C Company had been through two previous campaigns: Cape Gloucester on New Britain and Peleliu. Jerry shaped up and became one of the gutsiest men with whom we had ever served, earning a well-deserved Navy Cross for his bravery in the battle of Okinawa.

Jerry, though severely wounded, radioed C Company headquarters for help before we abandoned tank. We carried him up through the hatch. When we got him out, Jerry went into shock, so I took command of the four of us who survived. K. C. Smith, assistant driver and machine-gunner, and I put Jerry's arms over our shoulders and began carrying him across a field pockmarked by shells.

We headed back toward a pocket of Marines from the Seventh Regiment on Kunishi Ridge to our rear. We were still behind the Japanese front lines, so there were Japanese all around us. A hidden sniper drew a careful bead on us. He fired, cutting all three of us down with either one shot or a burst of machine-gun fire. K. C. was shot through the chin; Jerry was hit with a clean hole through the back of his neck; and I was shot through the neck—shattering my windpipe—and through my trigger finger. Three of us—an excellent shooting percentage! K. C. and the fourth man with us, escaped. I never saw either of them again.

Blood was running down the outside of my dungaree jacket, as well as down the inside of my throat. The agony of trying to breathe made me feel as if I were drowning. I was sure it was my time to die and that this was the bullet with my name on it.

"When it comes time to die, make sure all you have to do is die," is a wise saying. Do all of your soul preparation for that crucial, eternal moment. Get ready today, for tomorrow may be too late. Fortunately, I was ready.

My flesh was fearful, but my inner being experienced the peace of God that passes human understanding. The reason was that I had become a true Christian two years before on Goodenough Island, near New Guinea, by reading a pocket-sized Gideon New Testament.

With this excruciatingly painful injury and the tremendous loss of blood, I thought I was going to die. I rolled into a shell hole and tried to hurry the process by passing out; then I could go and be with the Lord. But I was unable to lose consciousness. As I lay there I began to realize that I may live. I decided to try to escape. Near death, I began to crawl and stumble across that desolate battlefield, expecting to feel another bullet crash into my body at any moment.

Jerry lay nearby. In my pitiful condition I was unable to help him. In a blurred glance before my escape, it looked as if he were dead. Later, I learned that enemy snipers in a nearby coral cave, with a well-concealed opening nearly flush with the ground, would shoot Jerry again and again. Four more bullets would tear into Jerry's body, in addition to his original thigh wound and the shot in the neck. But there was yet one more bullet to come in order for him to fully earn the nickname of "The Sieve."

The Miracle of the Red Sock

One of the few fully operational tanks of fifteen in C Company was commanded by Lt. Charlie Nelson. Hearing our earlier distress call on the radio, he came to the rescue. His gunner, mistaking Jerry Atkinson lying on the ground to be a Japanese, opened fire with his coaxial machine gun. As Jerry instinctively threw up his hand in a feeble protective effort, yet another bullet found him, smashing through his hand.

With most of his limbs incapacitated, Jerry, in a last ditch effort, began to wave his one good leg, which showed a red sock sticking up over the top of his combat boot. Charlie Nelson recognized the red sock and stopped the gunner, thus saving Jerry from certain death. Nelson's tank crew then risked their lives to secure the area and, along with advancing Marine infantry, rescued Jerry, carrying him out on a poncho.

As I stumbled out of what had once been an Okinawan sugar cane field, I came to a dirt road. It was here that I had to make a choice—go by way of the dirt road which eventually wound up on top of the ridge or try to go straight up the steep coral ridge to our own lines. If I went by way of the road—the longer way—I was fearful of running into enemy soldiers. Though I had a .45 caliber pistol on my hip, my trigger finger had been shattered and I couldn't draw or use the pistol.

My choice was to try to go straight up the ridge, but because of an extreme loss of blood, after only a few feet I had to stop. I couldn't go on. I sat helpless, holding my torn neck with my good left hand. I cried out to God for deliverance, but really believed this was the end of the line for me.

Just then Bud Brenkert's tank came out of the cane field where it had also been severely damaged by antitank fire. Scuddley Hoffman lay dead inside the tank. Because of this, Glen "Old Man" Christensen from Minnesota, at twenty-seven, one of the oldest men in the unit, was driving with his head out of the driver's hatch. Christensen spotted me, stopped, helped me onto the tank, then drove on to find medical help.

On top of Kunishi Ridge, a medical corpsmen, after treating my wounds as best he could, placed me on a stretcher on the back of Brenkert's tank. In order to reach the fishing village of Itoman, held by the Seventh Marine Regiment, we had to travel through a sniper-infested "no-man's valley." Brenkert, in a selfless act of courage, got out of the tank and stretched out across my weakened body to shield me from enemy fire. He risked his life to save mine.

But now this already damaged tank was unable to go any farther. It broke down in the middle of the sniper field. We were sitting targets! There were tense moments until Sergeant Brantly's tank rescued us and completed the evacuation.

Weeks later, I had an unexpected reunion at the San Francisco Receiving Hospital; Jerry "The Sieve" Atkinson was still alive. Both of us had thought that the other had been killed. What a tremendous reunion we had.

Would You Die for the Enemy?

There are two things that never change: One is the uncertainty of this life; the other is the certainty of death. Death is so final and we are helpless at its onslaught. Combat in wartime is a graphic, fast-forward microcosm of life in general. It reveals much in a short and frenetic period—discipline, training, camaraderie, suffering, sacrifice, and the wrenching finality of death.

I share these experiences in writing to pay tribute to these comrades from World War II, to all the men I served with in C Company and in the First Marine Division. All who survived are unforgettable men in unforgettable times. Their friendship, sacrifice, and camaraderie have marked my life to the end. We, the living, are grateful to each one who paid the supreme sacrifice. We salute them and our hearts go out to loved ones left behind.

At a small C Company reunion a few years after the war, D. I. Bahde, Nick Backovich, Olie Olson, Joe Alvarez, Bill Dunn, others, and I remembered those who had paid the supreme sacrifice. Many of the brave men in C Company are as close as brothers.

Along with these other Marines, Bud Brenkert and I had developed a camaraderie of over two years in three battles in the Pacific. This closeness through many dangers against a common enemy had created in Bud a willingness to sacrifice his life for mine. During that reunion, I publicly thanked Bud for his willingness to protect me when he placed his body on mine on the back of his tank.

At that emotional moment of thanksgiving, I asked Bud if he would have been willing to die for his enemy. He could not say "yes" and neither could I. Man's highest love is to die or be willing to die for a good friend or buddy.

But it has always amazed me that Jesus did just that—He died for His enemies. Before accepting Him as my Savior and Lord on Goodenough Island, I had been His enemy. God's love is so much greater than man's highest love. Romans 5:8 says, "God demonstrated His own love toward us, in that while we were yet sinners [or enemies], Christ died for us."

Because of the fateful events of 17 June 1945 described here, I continue to speak in a hoarse voice. Thousands of people throughout my lifetime have wondered, remarked about it, or asked how I contracted my "permanent" laryngitis. It was a small price to pay to serve our country with the men described here.

CITATION

The President of the United States takes pleasure in presenting the SILVER STAR MEDAL to SERGEANT CORNELIUS BRENKERT, UNITED STATES MARINE CORPS RESERVE, for service as set forth in the following CITATION:

For conspicuous gallantry and intrepidity while serving as a Tank Commander of Company C, First Tank Battalion, First Marine Division, in action against enemy Japanese forces on Okinawa, Ryukyu Islands, 17 June 1945. When his tank was hit four times and several of his crew members were seriously wounded by fire from an enemy antitank gun during an assault well forward of the front lines, Sergeant Brenkert observed that the tank of his Platoon Leader was disabled and on fire and, skillfully maneuvering his vehicle alongside the burning tank despite continuing hostile antitank fire, effected the rescue of its crew members. His outstanding courage and devotion to duty were in keeping with the highest traditions of the United States Naval Service. For the President, John L. Sullivan, Secretary of the Navy.

TWO

SPARKY

The Wounds of War Cannot Erase Hope

I have hope to live, and am prepar'd to die.
                        —*William Shakespeare, Measure for Measure*

C ombat on the sands of Iwo Jima was Sparky's one and only battle experience in the US Marine Corps. It cost him his eyes. I made three Marine Corps amphibious landings in the World War II Pacific Theater. My last battle, Okinawa, cost me my voice.

When I had been shot through the neck, the same bullet went through my trigger finger, shattering it beyond repair. It had to be amputated.

I first met Sparky in 1946 in the Philadelphia Naval Hospital. We were a beat-up pair, but between Sparky's voice and my eyes we got around ok. Many a time I was his hoarse, wheezing, seeing-eye dog those days in Philadelphia.

Shaking hands with Sparky was a kind of ritual. Because he was blind, he seemed to always need little signs of familiarity to reconfirm identities. In my case, even though he could tell me by my hoarse whisper, when we shook hands he always held my right hand in both of his hands. Then for several seconds he would carefully feel the stump of my right forefinger with the fingers of his left hand. Finally, he seemed to be satisfied it was really me.

There was no other name for this charismatic Marine but Sparky; it fit him perfectly. The moment he came into your presence you couldn't resist his contagious liveliness and humble charm. Even his sightless eyes seemed to sparkle. You liked him immediately.

Sparky had joined the Corps as a teenager. Thirsty for action, yet with some fear about the realities of combat, his path led toward the meat grinder of Iwo Jima.

The battle of Iwo began on February 19, 1945, and was the single bloodiest engagement of the war for the Marines, with 6,821 Marines and attached Navy personnel killed and 19,217 wounded. Approximately one out of every three Marines landing on Iwo became a casualty.

Sparky was one of them.

He was part of an artillery crew. Doggedly, his team fought their way inland against fanatical Japanese resistance. Sparky made it safely through the first day and night of horror on Iwo, in which 566 Marines and Navy corpsmen (medics) lay dead or dying on the black sands of the invasion beach. Robert Sherwood, the combat correspondent who landed with the Marines, said, *"The first night on Iwo can only be described as a nightmare in hell."*

A few days later Sparky met disaster. An incoming Japanese mortar shell knocked out Sparky's weapon and crew. He and several others were literally lifted off their feet and blown several yards through the air.

Iwo Jima became Sparky's personal "nightmare in hell" as he lay mangled and partially buried in the now blood-black sand. His whole body from the waist up was an agonizing, pitted mass of wounds. Mercifully, the shock of his extensive injuries caused him to pass in and out of consciousness.

The first corpsman to reach him audibly gasped when he saw Sparky's face and upper body. Though the medic had tended to many badly wounded and shattered men, he'd never seen anything like that. He thought Sparky would die and began to move away to tend other Marines, but an invisible hand seemed to hold him. He quickly went to work on the wounds. Then Sparky was evacuated and eventually ended up in the Philadelphia Naval Hospital.

When I first met Sparky in Philly, my eyes were riveted to his face. Small black pits pockmarked his face and neck. The exploding shell had driven the black volcanic sand into and under Sparky's skin. It was as if a drunken tattoo artist had been at work indiscriminately making his needle marks. For nearly a year the Naval surgeons removed as much of the imbedded black sand and shrapnel as possible, but they never got it all.

In spite of this, the will to survive surged in Sparky. He remained true to his nickname. Through innumerable transfusions and surgeries over the months, he slowly regained physical strength and emotional confidence in the midst of his dark, painful world. Both eyes were so badly damaged that the sockets were surgically removed. He was fitted with two prostheses that were a medical work of art. The dark brown color of these new eyes was so realistic that only the slight, backward tilt of Sparky's head when he talked to you gave away the secret that he was blind.

Sparky had long tenure in the Philadelphia Naval Hospital. He received numerous operations, studied Braille, and attended a downtown church. He fell in love with a girl named Virginia and asked her to marry him. I was his best man.

The big day came. As I guided him down the aisle to become one with a girl he had never seen, I thanked God for the privilege of knowing this physically sightless, but faith-filled, vibrant man. His hope, courage, and enthusiasm were contagious.

In early 1947, a few months after the wedding, I was discharged from the Marine Corps and returned to my home in Salem, Oregon. Over the next few years I kept track of Sparky through a mutual friend, Andy Kohan. One day in 1950, Andy wrote saying that Sparky had been readmitted and confined to a US Veteran's Hospital in Pennsylvania. It was Sparky's tragic lot in life to continue to suffer.

As soon as I could get the funds together and get a break from work, I headed for Philadelphia. Andy drove me to the Veteran's Hospital to see Sparky. I wasn't sure of the exact condition of my old buddy, but geared myself for the worst. I was not wrong in doing that. An orderly led us to a sun porch at the far end of the ward. Sparky was in a wheelchair. He made no response to my greetings, but faced blankly straight ahead.

The battle of Iwo Jima was slowly finishing its deadly business. The slivers of shrapnel and the thousands of tiny round pieces of volcanic sand that had taken out Sparky's eyes and disfigured his skin had also minutely pierced his brain. Though spinal meningitis had not taken his life, it did claim his speech and most of his memory.

Could this be the vibrant, tough, sightless comrade I had known? He was grossly overweight. He was not wearing his plastic eyes, so the two withered and wrinkled sunken holes in his face were lifeless. Where was the spark that had made us call him Sparky? I had a difficult time accepting the changes that had come into my buddy's life. I was dazed and felt helpless. Humanly speaking, there was no hope for Sparky. Could we even communicate? Could this friend who had vegetated into such a pitiful condition possibly recognize me?

As I spoke with him in my husky whisper, I took his right hand for a prolonged handshake. Slowly, his left hand came over and he began the ritual: As his right hand held mine, his left hand began to feel the nub of my missing right forefinger. He tried his best to speak, but made only unintelligible sounds. However, I knew that behind the layers of darkness there were shadows of recognition and response. My broken heart alternately rejoiced and despaired. I knew that I would probably never see Sparky again in this life.

I opened the Bible and read several portions to him, concluding with the incomparable King James version of Psalm 23:4, *"Yea, though I walk through the valley of the shadow of death, I will fear no evil; for thou art with me; thy rod and thy staff they comfort me."*

Sparky gripped my hand hard when I finished. He may not have had the outward exuberance of the Sparky of old, but I felt that inside he still had that spark of hope. I knew that this beautiful Psalm of power and comfort was reaching him. As I said goodbye to him, I hugged him and again he reached out to rub the stub of my forefinger.

Andy Kohan faithfully visited Sparky for over forty years. I received a letter from Andy about a year before God mercifully released Sparky from his pitiful state:

I visited Sparky a few days ago. He does not communicate or understand much. However, I notice if I sing a hymn, he will sing along with me. I have sat with him in my car and have turned on a Gospel program on the radio. He would nod his head in approval and point his finger up. When I mentioned the name of Jesus, he squeezed my hand and pointed upward. I don't think he remembers who I am, but I do seem to reach him with the hymns.

The other day I told him I had received a letter from you and asked him, 'Do you know Bob Boardman?' I was holding his hand at the time and he squeezed my hand and kept repeating your name.

Sparky's walk through the valley of the shadow of death was a painful, lonely, weary, and prolonged one. It eventually led him face to face with Jesus Christ, his Savior, whom he loved and worshiped despite the darkness of the shadows in the valley.

The eternal hope that overshadows the human sadness of Sparky's life is expressed well in these verses:

Therefore we are always confident and know that as long as we are at home in the body we are away from the Lord. We live by faith, not by sight. We are confident, I say, and would prefer to be away from the body and at home with the Lord. So we make it our goal to please him, whether we are at home in the body or away from it. (2 Cor. 5:6–9)

The following is etched on a granite monument on Iwo Jima, dedicated in English and Japanese:

REUNION OF HONOR
On the 40th Anniversary of
the Battle of Iwo Jima,
American & Japanese veterans met again on these same

sands, this time in peace and friendship. We commemorate our comrades, living and dead, who fought here with bravery & honor, and we pray together that our sacrifices on Iwo Jima will always be remembered and never be repeated.
February 19, 1985.
3rd, 4th, 5th Division Association,
USMC; and the [Japanese] Association of Iwo Jima

II. WAR AND LEAVING HOME . . . GUADALCANAL AND AUSTRALIA

THREE

"GOODBYE, DAD!"

Hard Decisions in Unforgettable Times—a Teenager Goes Off to War

> Decision is a sharp knife that cuts clean and straight; indecision is a dull one that hacks and tears and leaves ragged edges behind it.
>
> *—Gordon Graham*

World War II was one year old when I turned 18, and I bid my dad goodbye in Salem, Oregon. We boarded a city bus to go down to the train station together where I would join other recruits on that long journey to Southern California. Sitting up on a train all the way to San Diego seemed like riding in style to most of us who had rarely ridden a train.

There on that Salem city bus it was somewhat awkward and painful riding with my dad, but it was comforting to have him see me off. My mom wouldn't go with us because of the emotional trauma of saying goodbye. I had wanted to join the Marines right after Pearl Harbor, to get in on the action and excitement, but in those days if you were under 18, both parents had to sign release papers and my mom wouldn't sign.

All the way to the train depot, I kept trying to think of what to say to my dad on that final goodbye that would give him confidence that I was not afraid to go off to war. Finally, I had an inspirational thought—something out of an old James Cagney or Humphrey Bogart movie. As I shook hands for the final time I put on my best tough-guy act and said, "Goodbye, Dad! I'll be back!" However, I don't think my false bravado fooled him.

Every man's relationship to his earthly father is so important. The older we get, the more we realize that we are who we are because of our relationship—or lack of a relationship—to our fathers. I once read where movie actor Kirk Douglas spent his whole life trying to gain his father's approval and affirmation for his accomplishments in the movies, but never could. He did, I believe, carry this deep regret and heartache to the grave.

Looking back in my own life, I appreciated my dad, but we weren't really close. At the train depot as we said goodbye, we didn't hug, just shook hands. Today my younger brother, Tom, and I can't remember Dad ever showing us a lot of fatherly affection. It seems as though he didn't know how to foster a close relationship with us, though we know he loved us. He would occasionally take us on walks—and he was quite generous. If I'd ask him for a nickel, he would often give a dime or quarter.

The last time I said "Goodbye, Dad," was when my father died. His dying process took three months through a series of about eight cerebral strokes. I took a leave of absence from work and took care of him at home. I had become a Christian in the Marine Corps. Dad opposed my faith up until the time of his terminal illness.

My father was a good upright citizen, World War I veteran, YMCA worker, Rotarian, and church member, but had never personally embraced Jesus Christ as his Lord and Savior. On his deathbed in 1951, I took care of his physical needs, but also ministered to the deep inner spiritual needs of his slowly ebbing life.

Day after day I read him the message of hope from the Bible. He personally acknowledged Christ as Savior five weeks before his death at the age of sixty-nine. As I told him goodbye for the final time, I am confident that because of the mercy, love, and grace of Jesus Christ, we will someday meet again in God's presence.

All of this reminds me that two thousands years ago Jesus Christ said, "Goodbye, Father," as He left the glories of heaven to come to earth and give Himself as a sinless, perfect sacrifice for us. It must have been very difficult to part from His Heavenly Father, because of the close bonds between them from eternity. Their love for us compelled them to part for a season.

For those who have estranged relationships with earthly fathers or other loved ones, with little or no hope of reconciliation, there is hope. The Father in heaven can meet all of those unfulfilled earthly needs by becoming a personal Father to us through His Son, Jesus Christ.

That spiritual relationship gives the basis for mending and restoring earthly ones that have been cracked or sometimes hopelessly alienated. If God gets all the pieces of a broken, shattered heart, He is an expert in putting those pieces back together.

FOUR

THE RECUITERS

Seven Recruiting Qualities

You will not see an advertisement that says anything about a college fund. You will not see one that says we will give you a skill. All we say is, do you want to be challenged physically, mentally, and morally? Join the Marine Corps and we'll guarantee you'll be changed, and the change will be forever. That's our commercial.

—Four-star Gen. Charles Krulak,
31st Commandant of the US Marine Corps

The airmail letter from my best buddy was marked "Guadalcanal" and was written on captured Japanese stationery. It was still 1942, the early days of World War II. My best friend from high school, Warren Ling, had enlisted in the Marine Corps at age seventeen, just a few months before the attack on Pearl Harbor. Now he was in action on Guadalcanal, the first Marine amphibious campaign during World War II, which was on the radio and in the newspapers daily.

After hearing those combat reports and getting the letters from Warren, I went to the Marine Corps office in my hometown of Salem, Oregon. That's when I met the Marine recruiter, Sergeant Ringland, who was immaculate in his dress blues and the epitome of how a USMC recruiter should appear.

He enhanced the legend of the Corps, as I came with other young men from around that area to enlist. We not only hoped for the excitement and adventure of combat, but also for the same sharpness of bearing and appearance. The Marines promised to make men out of green, undisciplined youths; I wanted that.

41

I'll never forget that conversation with Sergeant Ringland. He asked me if I wanted to sign up as a Regular or as a Reserve. I had no idea what that meant. He explained: "A Regular Marine signs on for four years. A Reserve for the duration of the war plus six months. Take your choice." His pen was poised, waiting for my answer.

As an eighteen-year old, I had never made a decision like that affecting my life so far into the future. "Sergeant Ringland, could I go over in that corner and think about this matter for a few minutes before I give you my answer?"

In the corner of the Marine recruiting office I mulled over these options. Four years sounded like forever to me, so finally I returned to the sergeant and told him that my choice was to become a Reserve.

As it finally turned out, I served in the Marine Corps for four years and two months!

Sergeant Ringland not only recruited me but also his own son, David, as well. After David and I were sworn in we left Salem by train for San Diego, where we went through boot camp in the same platoon. Tragically, David was later killed in combat on Bougainville in the Solomon Islands. It must have been particularly painful for his father, especially after personally recruiting his own son.

Meet another Marine recruiter. He is Ron York, originally from Kellogg, Idaho, one of my best buddies. Although we served in the Marines at different times, we both joined as teenagers. Ron spent four years in the Corps from 1950–1954. A few months after enlisting, he landed in Korea on a cold Christmas Day, 1950, as a miserable replacement for A Company First Battalion, Seventh Marine Regiment, First Marine Division.

On York's way to Korea in his replacement battalion, he met a wounded Marine in Japan returning to the United States. Ron mentioned that his birthday was coming up soon. He would just be turning eighteen. This salty veteran of the hard, no-quarter fighting on the Korean peninsula offered Ron some cynical encouragement: "Buddy, you'll never see your next birthday!"

Ron was in combat in Korea's rugged and often freezing terrain for one year. Wounded in the right arm by North Korean hand grenade fragments, he was evacuated to a Navy hospital ship for treatment for two weeks. Then back into the battle.

For exploits in combat and superb leadership as a rifleman, York was decorated with the Silver Star, our nation's third highest award for valor. Subsequently, he became a Marine recruiter in Seattle and then in Northern Idaho. At the end of his recruiting duty in July 1954, "Sergeant York," had an overall average of 130 percent above his assigned quota. In one sense, the Marine Corps is only as good as its recruiters, so it is important that these men who replenish the Corps be above average.

York recently shared some keys to recruiting a few good men:

1. Attitude is everything. A successful recruiter loves the Corps and it shows in his positive outlook.
2. Appearance must be sharp.
3. Experience breeds confidence. Ron had been in battle. No one can gainsay that personal experience.
4. Appeal to potential recruits as men. Let them know there will be a price to pay in training and in combat. The Marines don't want or need the thundering herd—just a few good men.
5. Focus on the task. Don't let the good sidetrack you from the best. Don't get entangled in civilian affairs, but seek to please the one who recruits you.
6. Be persistent. Never, never give up on potential recruits. Don't go strictly by outward appearance, but try to see what that man may eventually become.
7. Have a good strategy. Reach one and through him recruit others.

There is another recruiter I met in the Marine Corps who unexpectedly impacted my life as no one else has ever done. I never thought that in the midst of such a gung ho, macho outfit, I would ever encounter Him. He was Jesus Christ. I heard His name everywhere and also used His name in vain, but never thought I would meet Him face to face.

He was a man among men. So unassuming, yet so dynamic. I read about Him in a Gideon-issued New Testament for the first time, as the First Marine Division moved from Australia by ship into the South Pacific. I found that He was absolutely the most fascinating, amazing, and fearless person who ever walked this earth. The more I learned about Him, the more I wanted to know Him personally and follow Him at any price.

Just as He recruited the twelve renegades in the gospels who eventually, minus Judas, became the apostles, he spoke to me and, gently, but firmly, let me know that He would change my messed-up life and give me hope. He not only gave me hope, forgiveness of sins and eternal heart peace, but also promised me a new task wherever I went.

As Jesus challenged one of the most unlikely of His recruits, Matthew the tax collector, who worked for the hated Romans, He also said to me, *"Follow me and I will make you a fisher [or recruiter] of men"* (Matt. 4:19). I am unworthy to be called His servant and have failed Jesus Christ many times. He has never once failed me.

In reading the seven points on successful recruiting above, Jesus Christ more than fulfills each one in our warfare of daily life. He is the Recruiter of all recruiters. He still works at recruiting people day and night.

To each of us He says, *"Come unto me, all you that labor and are heavy laden, and I will give you rest"* (Matt. 11:28)

THE NAME

What's in a Name?

A name is a kind of face whereby one is known.

—*Fuller*

One of the unique things about serving in the US Marine Corps is that so many Marines have nicknames. Often, one that fits exactly. The close quarters of living, training, eating, and fighting a war together brings a keen knowledge of one another.

And it starts in boot camp.

Platoon 1182, number 506095. Like most Marines I can never forget my boot camp platoon and serial number. A few tent rows away scuttlebutt had it that movie actor Tyrone Power was also a boot. Some of us sneaked over to try to spot him. His name and career evoked our curiosity. No luck.

Other names began to come into our awareness in boot camp. The crucial battle of Guadalcanal had just ended in the Solomon Islands. The First Marine Division and elements of the Second, plus a US Army outfit, had stopped the Japanese on land in their southwestern thrust toward Australia and New Zealand. The US Navy, though suffering heavy losses in ships and personnel, inflicted devastating strikes against the Imperial Japanese Navy.

In boot camp, and afterwards in infantry and tank training, we began to hear names like Mitch Paige, John Basilone, "Red Mike" Edson, A. A. Vandergrift, Barney Ross, Chesty Puller, Lou Diamond, Pappy Boyington, and others. Many of these became legends in their day and several paid the supreme price. These are worthy names and ones to be honored for their exploits.

In C Company, First Tank Battalion, First Marine Division, we had our share of outstanding characters. When it was learned that the guy with a large handlebar mustache was from Montana, he was immediately dubbed "Sheepherder." Glen Christensen from Minneapolis, at age twenty-seven, was "Old Man," because he was five to ten years older than most of us. He was also called "Banty Rooster," a feisty little guy who backed down from no man, friend or foe.

Two men from C Company's maintenance platoon who seemed to do everything together were Brown and Beutow. They became "Bread and Butter." A weightlifter of Polish descent was, of course, "Muscles," or "Ski." Another of my closest buddies, Joe Alvarez— wounded on Okinawa in the "Father's Day Massacre" on Kunishi Ridge on 17 June 1945—had a proverbial million-dollar smile. He was "Pearls."

A close comrade out of Jacques Farm in San Diego, Donald Irving Bahde, became "D. I." (Drill Instructor), just because of his initials, for he wasn't really a drill instructor. When he and I first joined C Company in Australia as replacements in mid-1943, our chunky, rosy-cheeked sergeant and tank commander was Durbin. We soon dubbed him "Deana" (after a singer and actress of that era), but never to Durbin's face; D. I. and I were lowly privates.

Then there was "Pack-up" Paposkas (not his real name). When he had enough points from being overseas, he was overly eager to return to the United States. He was packed and ready to depart. Many times a day on Pavuvu, he would scan the bulletin board in front of the office tent to see if his name was there. "Pack-up" was a parade-ground Marine.

One of the most unforgettable men in C Company was our executive officer in the battle of Okinawa, Walter "MuMu" Moore. His nickname was unforgettable and to know him was an experience. A great career Marine, a veteran of three wars, and recipient of two Silver Stars, he had contracted a case of filariasis while in Samoa. From then on he was "MuMu."

"Pinky" Pinkston from Oklahoma had a Japanese grenade explode almost between his legs on Peleliu and wasn't scratched. He repented on the spot. "Guts" Gifford earned his name not so much from prowess in combat, but from the visible results of many trips to the slop chute, or bar.

"Scuddly" Hoffman, just eighteen, the ridge runner from Virginia, was killed in the Father's Day Massacre. The C Company nicknames seem endless: "Olie" Olson; "Frenchy" Renard; "Buzz" Barwick; "Pop" Sims; and Jerry "The Sieve" Atkinson, because he was wounded seven times in the Massacre and is still alive today in Tennessee. C Company also had "Red" Saunders, Tom "Dud" Duddleson, and "Wild Bill" Henahan.

Other tankers include "Pappy" Gore of B Company, a macho Pappy Yokum type. "Roughhouse" Taylor (yes, he was), "Slopeplate" McDonald, Joe "Spike" Malcolm, Tom "Whiskey" Hughes (a non-drinker), "Uncle" Phil Morell, and the outstanding First Tank Battalion commander, Arthur "Jeb" Stuart.

The great majority of these warrior-characters did an outstanding job for their country and the Corps. Many shed their blood and were deservedly decorated.

But there is a name far more well known in the US Marine Corps than any of the above named men of action and bravery. As soon as I came into the Corps, I heard his name daily—many, many times a day! He was spoken of in the most unexpected places: in mess halls and tents, on drill fields, in card games, in the slop chute, in training exercises, and onboard ship. Amazingly, I heard this name in combat, too!

His name is Jesus Christ. I brought His name with me into the Corps like thousands of other young men. I picked up this strange and thoughtless habit of taking His name in vain as a preteen. By the time we shipped overseas as the Seventeenth Replacement Battalion in 1943 on the old *USS Rochambeau* and integrated into the First Marine Division, I was quite adept at using this name in vain in many different ways.

The New Testament says that the name of Jesus Christ is the name that is above every name and that someday every knee shall bow before him and every tongue shall confess that Jesus is Lord, to the glory of God the Father (Phil. 2:9–10). I used this exalted and priceless name in vain as a young Marine to express anger, sorrow, for emphasis, in joking, in frustration, and even to show happiness.

Every one of us, with few exceptions, will say about Jesus Christ that He was either the Son of God, or at the least, a very good man. If so, why do we use that matchless name so carelessly and vainly?

Why not swear with the names of well-known people such as Dwight Eisenhower, Pope John Paul, Mother Teresa, Chesty Puller, or Billy Graham? We can all smile for we know that though highly respected, there is no power in these names when used to swear by. But the name of Jesus Christ is unique, powerful, and is above any name in heaven or on earth. It must grieve Him to hear His name used so lightly and vainly.

My purpose in saying this is not to crusade against swearing, but to think about the name of Jesus Christ, perfect God, equal with the Father. He is also a perfect, sinless man who died in our place on the cross. When the curtain comes down and our number comes up, Jesus Christ is the one who holds the power of eternal life. The Bible also tells us that He will judge the whole earth. He is the creator of the universe.

In the Bible the Lord God is referred to by over four hundred names, with more than one hundred of those applying to Jesus Christ. Jesus means *God the Savior.* Christ means the *Anointed of God.* Together the two words mean *He who is God and as such is able to save us from our sins.* He lives today as the Resurrected One.

Perhaps you have been thoughtlessly taking this priceless name in vain, as I once did. He is long suffering and merciful, still open to our sincere cry for help. The name that is above every name in heaven and in earth can be our refuge, hope, and Savior.

"Hallowed be Your name."

Signed—Murphy, Murph, Bangs, Boardy.

SIX

A FEW GOOD MEN
Small Matches Light Great Torches

Take all of my factories, all of my business—all but my men—
and I'll build again.

—*Andrew Carnegie*

The United States Marine Corps has been fortunate to produce
outstanding leadership throughout its over 221-year history.
Through selection, training, discipline, and the giving of responsibility, the Corps has taken American patriots and molded them
into one of the world's finest fighting cadres. Man for man, pound
for pound, most Marines believe they can match and defeat any
foe. In most cases that instilled *esprit* lasts a lifetime.

Wartime accelerates both the need for good leadership and the
potential for finding it. During World War II we came out of small
towns, off the farms, from big cities, through a seven-week boot
camp, and into training units.

Alvarez, Aden, Bahde, Backovich, Barwick, Brenkert, and
Christensen—we were all privates and were "volunteered" for tanks
alphabetically. We didn't make PFC until after our first campaign
on Cape Gloucester. As lowly privates it was hard to tell by our
looks and actions that there was any leadership present. But by the
time the battle of Okinawa took place, those men were some of the
heart and soul of leadership in C Company. They were tank commanders, drivers, and gunners—all battle-tested and several decorated for bravery.

Finding and choosing excellent leaders is a fine and difficult
art. In the Marine Corps, or in any walk of life, it is easy to make

49

the wrong choice, to judge by outward appearances, and to overlook hidden leadership potential. The following "memo," author unknown, illustrates this:

TO: Jesus, son of Joseph
        Woodcrafters Carpenter Shop
        Nazareth 25922

FROM: Jordan Management Consultants
        Jerusalem 26544

Dear Sir,

Thank you for submitting the resumes of the twelve men you have picked for management positions in your new organization. All of them have now taken our battery of tests and we have not only run the results through our computer, but also arranged personal interviews for each of them with our psychologist and vocational aptitude consultant.

The profiles of all tests are included, and you will want to study each of them carefully.

As part of our service and for your guidance, we make some general comments, much as an auditor will include some general statement. This is given as a result of staff consultation and comes without any additional fee.

It is the staff opinion that most of your nominees are lacking in background, education, and vocational aptitude for the type of enterprise you are undertaking. They do not have a team concept. We would recommend that you continue your search for persons of experience in managerial ability and proven capability.

Simon Peter is emotionally unstable and given to fits of temper. Andrew has absolutely no qualities of leadership. The two brothers, James and John, the sons of Zebedee, place personal interest above company policy. Thomas demonstrates a questioning attitude that would tend to undermine morale. We feel that it is our duty to tell you that Matthew has been blacklisted by the Greater Jerusalem Better Business Bureau. James, the son of Alphaeus, and Thaddaeus definitely have radical leanings, and they both registered a high score on the manic-depressive scale.

One of the candidates, however, shows great potential. He is a man of ability and resourcefulness, meets people well, has a keen business mind and has contacts in high places. He is highly motivated, ambitious and responsible. We recommend Judas Iscariot as your comptroller and right-hand man. All of these other profiles are self-explanatory.

We wish you every success in your new venture.

Sincerely,
Jordan Management Consultants

This imaginative tongue-in-cheek memo is not far removed from the way the modern world today views Jesus Christ's choice of potential leaders. But Jesus made no mistake in His choice of men who would turn the world upside down.

Just as the Marine Corps enlisted, trained, and brought Alvarez, Bahde, Backovich, Barwick, Brenkert, Christensen, and many others space forbids me to name, to become leaders who helped win battles and defeat a tenacious enemy, so Jesus chose and developed over time His potential band of men.

The disciples were humanly unlikely candidates. As the memo states, they did lack in background, education, and vocational aptitude. They failed in certain areas of their apprenticeship. Jesus Christ could well have given up on them. But He didn't.

After Christ's resurrection and ascension into heaven, those motley men went into all the world proclaiming His deity! People responded by placing personal faith in this Good News, and we are here today as a result of their leadership. Jesus Christ sees the potential in every one of our lives.

"When they saw the courage of Peter and John and realized that they were unschooled, ordinary men, they were astonished and they took note that those men had been with Jesus" (Acts 4:13).

SEVEN

GUADALCANAL MACHINE GUNNER MITCH PAIGE'S HIGHEST HONOR

Lonely Courage

I am only one, but I am one. I can't do everything, but I can do something. And what I can do, I ought to do. And what I ought to do, by the Grace of God, I shall do.

—*Edward E. Hale*

When Platoon Sergeant Mitchell Paige landed on Guadalcanal in 1942, there was no ridge named "Paige's Hill" on that jungle island, but there is now.

Yet that wasn't his highest honor.

As a Platoon Sergeant landing with thousands of other enlisted men, Paige never thought he would become an officer. But he earned a battlefield commission to Second Lieutenant.

Yet, that wasn't his highest honor.

When Paige's platoon carried their machine guns through the surf onto the sands of Guadalcanal, he never dreamed his courage with that weapon would earn him the Congressional Medal of Honor for heroism in combat, the highest award an American can earn in wartime, but he earned one.

Yet even that wasn't Mitch Paige's highest honor.

Guadalcanal—mysterious tropical island of swaying coconut palms, coral beaches, sluggish, fungus-laden streams, and nearly impenetrable, hostile jungle. A place where malaria was as deadly as combat. Only 90 miles long and 26 miles wide, this key island in the British Solomon group, 700 miles east of New Guinea, was a strategic battleground in the first year of World War II. The airfield on Guadalcanal was essential for American use to further penetrate Japanese-held territory.

On August 7, 1942, the First Marine Division Reinforced (956 officers and 18,146 enlisted) made their historic landing on the Canal. Together with elements of the Second Marine Division and later reinforced by US Army units, the First endured a four-month slugfest, sometimes in hand-to-hand jungle combat against 40,000 wily, tenacious Japanese soldiers. The victory was hard won, with over 1,700 US Marines, Navy Corpsmen and soldiers killed. The Japanese were only able to eventually evacuate about 10,000 troops. Over 5,000 American sailors perished in crucial offshore sea battles.

During the first weeks of battle there, the question often asked on the home front was, "Can our Marines hold?" For we had discovered that the Japanese were a formidable foe, who would fight to the death. The motto of one of the Japanese Regiments, the 29th Infantry, was: *remember that Death is lighter than a feather, but that Duty is heavier than a mountain.*

However, this fanatical enemy had underestimated the American courage, determination, and ability to fight. In post-war interviews, Japanese officers concluded that "the losses suffered in the Solomons weakened all subsequent Japanese defensive efforts and reduced Japanese naval air strength to a point from which it was never to recover." Captain Ohmae, the Japanese naval planner who helped strategize the Solomons campaign, told US interrogators after the war, "After Guadalcanal I knew we could not win the war. I did not think we would lose, but I knew we could not win."

After the landing on Guadalcanal, the Marines unexpectedly and quickly captured the Japanese-built airfield and named it Henderson Field after Major Loften R. Henderson, a USMC pilot who was killed in the Battle of Midway in June 1942. After that tactical defeat the Japanese put ferocious effort and manpower into recapturing the airfield and in trying to drive US forces from the island.

Pivotal to winning back the airfield would be capturing the high ground around the strip, especially one of the key ridges, which had been taken by Mitch Paige's decimated platoon of marines armed with heavy, water-cooled thirty-caliber machine guns and other weapons. Mitch was part of H Company, Second Battalion, Seventh Regiment, First Marine Division. Previous casualties and malaria had reduced Mitch's original forty-eight-man platoon down to thirty-three. Though they had taken the hill, they were under clear observation by Japanese spotters on Mt. Austen. Artillery fire from the mountain had already shattered E Company, which was on the west flank of Mitch's machine gun platoon. The battle on Paige's Hill on October 26, 1942 was one of the crucial combat engagements that prevented the enemy from recapturing Henderson Field.

Mitch says, "Throughout the daylight hours of October 25, we continued checking and rechecking our rifles, pistols, machine guns, bayonets, knives, and ammunition—and waited with some apprehension for night to fall. We knew that the enemy was aware of our position. All that day, the Imperial Navy sent warships down from Rabaul, New Britain to shell our positions.

"Our outfit considered themselves the best machine gunners in the entire Corps. We were all in top physical and mental condition, despite a general prevalence of malaria. Long periods of training together coupled with the fact that all my guns were equipped with our beloved 'Mahoney System,' as I used to call it, gave us all confidence." Captain Mahoney, with Mitch's assistance, had modified the weapons to make them fire more effectively and twice as fast.

Marine patrols reported that just prior to midnight a large body of enemy troops was beginning to move toward the ridge. These comprised two battalions of the Japanese 124th Infantry Regiment and one battalion of the 4th Regiment. They were now fulfilling their unit motto about death and duty.

Mitch and his understrength platoon knew that they must hold the ridge at any cost. If the hill were lost, Henderson field would be lost—and that airfield was the reason they were on the island. Mitch moved up and down the line encouraging every man. All machine gun and rifle fire was to be held until the enemy could be seen.

Mitch said, "At about 0200 on 26 October, in a silence so pervasive that men many yards apart could hear each other breathe, I began to sense movement all along the front. Deep in the jungles below us we could hear the muffled clanking of equipment and, periodically, voices hissing in Japanese. These were undoubtedly squad leaders giving their instructions."

The battle erupted simultaneously for both sides. Hand grenades were hurled toward the jungle edge by the Marines as the enemy began their charge up the hill. Rifle and machine gun fire crisscrossed in deadly enfilading fire. Captain Louis Ditta's 60mm mortars exploded into the attacking masses of enemy soldiers no more than thirty yards beyond the Marine lines.

Some of the enemy gained the top of the ridge and were now in Marine positions. It became a series of small life and death struggles over the entire ridge top. Bayonets and two-handed Samurai swords flashed. The survivors of the first wave of Japanese attackers failed, but were soon followed by a second assault. All of Mitch Paige's remaining thirty-three men were either killed or wounded, but the wounded who were able kept on fighting.

The second enemy wave was crawling all over the hill and just before dawn was very close to controlling the ridge. Manning one of the guns, Paige described the action:

> I continued to trigger bursts until the barrel began to steam. In front of me was a large pile of dead bodies. Spent cartridge shells cluttered the area all around my gun. I ran along the ridge from gun to gun trying to keep them firing, but at each emplacement I found only dead bodies. I knew then that I must be alone. As I ran back and forth, I bumped into enemy soldiers who seemed to dash aimlessly in the dark. Apparently they weren't aware that they had almost complete possession of this hill.

One enemy soldier, slightly off-balance, thrust his bayonet at Mitch. The point nicked two of Mitch's fingers, but Mitch parried aside the thrust and then killed the soldier with his K-bar knife.

In the midst of the raging battle, Mitch Paige acknowledged the Providence of the living God in sparing his life time after time. A few minutes after the bayonet attack, Mitch and an enemy soldier raced to an unmanned Marine machine gun. Paige got there first, discovered the weapon was unloaded and frantically tried to load it. He said:

> Suddenly, a very strange feeling came over me. I tried desperately to reach forward and pull the bolt handle back to load the gun. But I felt as though my body was in a vise. Even so, I was completely relaxed and felt as though I was sitting peaceful in a park. Then all of a sudden I felt a release effect and I fell forward over the gun, loaded it, and swung the weapon around, aiming it at the enemy gunner, aware, as I did, of a strange sensation.
>
> At the precise moment that I had been unable to move, the enemy had fired his full 30-round magazine at me. I felt the heat and thrust of those bullets pass close to my chin and neck. If I had made the natural move forward with my head and arm for the necessary second pull of the bolt handle, the enemy bullets would have ripped through my head.
>
> For days I thought about this mystery and somehow I knew that God also knew what happened. *Boy, that guy had me cold . . . he really had me cold! Thank you, Lord, you really pulled me out of that one. You know, Lord, you put up that shield or something to make that guy miss me.*

As dawn broke on October 26, Paige rallied a ragtag band of Marines from various platoons for a final assault down the front slope of the hill against the surviving enemy. Cradling a water-cooled, but red-hot machine gun in his bare arms, and firing from the waist, Mitch and this cadre of men finished the task.

A few weeks later, Major General A. A. Vandergrift, commander of the First Marine Division, commended Platoon Sgt. Paige, "Son, that was an important hill that you and your men held. It was the last major Japanese effort to dislodge us and capture the airstrip."

At Mount Martha, in Victoria, Australia, several months after the crucial battle for Guadalcanal, four men were decorated with the Congressional Medal of Honor, our nation's highest award. The men were General Vandergrift, Col. Mike Edson, Sgt. John Basilone, and the now Second Lieutenant Mitchell Paige, who had received a battlefield commission. Mitch made the Corps a career and retired on November 1, 1959 as full colonel.

The President of the United States takes pleasure in presenting the CONGRESSIONAL MEDAL OF HONOR to PLATOON SERGEANT MITCHELL PAIGE, USMC, for service set forth in the following CITATION:

"For extraordinary heroism and conspicuous gallantry in action above and beyond the call of duty while serving with the Second Battalion, Seventh Marines, First Marine Division, in combat against enemy Japanese forces in the Solomon Islands Area on October 26, 1942. When the enemy broke through the line directly in front of his position, Platoon Sergeant Paige, commanding a machine gun section with fearless determination, continued to direct the fire of his gunners until all his men were either killed or wounded. Alone, against the deadly hail of Japanese shells, he manned his gun, and when it was destroyed, took over another, moving from gun to gun, never ceasing his withering fire against the advancing hordes until reinforcements finally arrived. Then, forming a new line, he dauntlessly and aggressively led a bayonet charge, driving the enemy back and preventing a break-through in our lines. His great personal valor and unyielding devotion to duty were in keeping with the highest traditions of the United States Naval Service."

Franklin Delano Roosevelt
President, United States

Anyone who receives the Congressional Medal of Honor (MOH) is stamped as a true hero. They are feted for the rest of their lives. Of this high honor, Mitch says, "I've been asked many times about having the Congressional Medal of Honor. I don't know what other men say, but I know in my own heart that it's just like being on a ball team. No one man wins these things. Since Guadalcanal days, I've said that probably the greatest heroes, the real MOH men, were the ones that nobody ever knew about.

"They died out there somewhere saving their buddies, probably performing an act that was well beyond the call of duty, and nobody ever knew about it . . . and they probably outnumber all the Medal of Honor people we've ever had in our country. Yet none of them have ever been recognized. But in my book, they're the heroes. That's the way I've always felt. I know what people say when they read 'alone' in my MOH citation. I say, 'No, I had 33 men. A piece of my medal belongs to every man in my platoon.'"

When Mitchell Paige left home in McKeesport, PA to enlist in the Marines on September 1, 1936, his God-fearing mother admonished him, "Just trust in God always." Six years later, right after the battle for Paige's Hill, Mitch emptied the contents of his combat pack and because of burned hands cradling the machine gun, gingerly picked up his small pocket Gideon New Testament which also contained Psalms and Proverbs.

He opened to Proverbs 3 and read *"Trust in the Lord with all your heart, and lean not on your own understanding; in all your ways acknowledge him, and he will make your paths straight."* This was Mitch's guiding principle through the war and for the rest of his life.

Mitchell Paige's greatest earthly honor was being awarded the Congressional Medal of Honor. But he places this award in its proper perspective, *"My greatest honor, bar none, is, as a sinner, to know Jesus Christ as my Lord and Savior and through Him to know the heart peace that passes all human understanding."*

EIGHT

I FOUGHT THE BATTLE OF BALLARAT AND LOST

Unexpected Consequences

Man's extremity is God's opportunity.

—*John Flavel*

A fistfight, a broken window, some stolen shoelaces, and a Gideon-issued New Testament started me on my spiritual odyssey.

It was June 1943. I was part of a replacement contingent of two battalions of Marines sent to Australia to join up with the Guadalcanal veterans of the First Marine Division.

As a typical young Marine, I was searching for adventure and action, not for deep spiritual truths. Stamped on the metal dog-tags around my neck were my name, serial number, blood type and the letter "P." This meant "Protestant," but was there simply because I wasn't a Catholic. It meant virtually nothing, since I claimed to be an atheist. I had absolutely no interest in spiritual matters. I was a "dog-tag Christian"—in name on metal only!

Young men make the best combat troops because they are filled with enthusiasm, a sense of adventure, and don't ask too many deep questions—especially about death and dying, unless it is just before battle.

Although I had occasionally attended church as a youth, I had never read the Bible. And I don't remember anyone ever explaining it to me. But when we boarded the *USS Rochambeau* in San

Diego heading for Australia, the Red Cross workers gave each Marine a small "ditty" bag of personal items, one of which was a Gideon's New Testament, with Psalms and Proverbs. We tucked these little bags in with our combat gear.

After landing at Melbourne, we took a train about one hundred miles northwest to the peaceful inland town of Ballarat which had a population of about twenty thousand. From the train station we were taken by trucks to Victoria Memorial Park, where my unit—C Company, First Tank Battalion, First Marine Division—was quartered in eight-man tents.

Australia had been in the war since 1939. Most of her able-bodied men were either in North Africa, New Guinea, or POW camps. By the end of World War II over twenty-seven thousand had died in combat. In and around Ballarat we encountered the Home Guard, made up of older men, a few Diggers (the nickname for Aussie soldiers) on leave, and some members of the Royal Australian Air Force.

Although we wouldn't have our first combat experience until December 26, 1943, at Cape Gloucester on the east end of the island of New Britain, I was itching for action . . . now!

D. I. Bahde from Kearney, Nebraska, a close buddy, and I went out one afternoon for a pub-crawl. The more we drank the bolder we became. We were ready for combat and decided to test our skills on some Aussies. The Battle of Ballarat was about to begin.

As Bahde and I passed several Diggers standing in front of a butcher shop, we imagined that they had made some smart aleck remarks, and turned to challenge them. At first we stood face to face with the Diggers, daring them to repeat their slurs. But I hadn't joined the Marines to talk. I wanted action, so I swung at the nearest Aussie. He ducked. I missed him, and my hand went through the plate glass window of the butcher shop.

The glass exploded. It seemed that the sound could be heard all over town, so Bahde and I took off, knowing the police would arrive soon. The first indication of any problem was the feeling of something warm flowing down my hand. Then I saw the gaping wound. I had severed the tendons in my right hand. In one wild swing, my combat on the streets of Ballarat came to a swift end and I wondered if my Marine Corps experience would also be over.

The bobbies (police) had been alerted. They stopped us and asked for identification. I tried to hide my wounded hand behind my back, but it was no use. The Marine military police arrived, and I was taken to Australian Military Hospital #88. The doctors operated immediately, tying the tendons together before they drew up into my arm which would leave my hand useless. My wrist and arm were immobilized in a plaster cast.

When I awakened from the effects of the ether anesthetic, I saw wounded and malaria-infected Diggers from the New Guinea battlefield in beds all around me. They merited the hospital space and medical attention, but here I was, a nineteen-year-old, green-horn Marine who had never been in combat, taking up undeserved space because of a disgraceful fight with one of their mates. I felt the most miserable I'd ever been in my life. I was sure these men would ostracize me because of my foolish brawl.

Contrary to my fears, they befriended me! I learned about the Diggers' famous "mateship." I couldn't use my right hand, so they tied my shoelaces and cut my meat at mealtimes. They accepted me as a "cobber" (a buddy), and their kindnesses humiliated me all the more.

I was also deeply concerned about whether I would ever be able to use my arm and hand again. To me it would have been the disgrace of my life if I hadn't been able to rejoin my unit and go into combat with them. I would have lost face and honor, not only before C Company, but also before my family, friends, and the whole nation. I was deeply, desperately concerned. This uncertainty about my future and the feeling of shame were two key elements that caused me to begin to seek God. But there was a third factor that added to my guilt.

The very afternoon before I put my fist through the window, the heel had come off my shoe. Bahde and I went to a cobbler shop and while the cobbler kindly repaired my shoe—free of charge because I was a Marine—I stole some shoelaces and shoe polish from the front of his shop.

Lying in my hospital bed I could see my uniform hanging on the wall with the pockets bulging with stolen goods. I was really the heel that needed repairing. My miseries increased. It is often the seemingly insignificant events in life that awaken our spiritual lethargy.

During one of Bahde's visits to the hospital, I asked him to bring me the New Testament in the little Red Cross ditty bag in my gear at the tank battalion. It had always been available to read, but because of the indulgences of the flesh and the spiritual darkness of my mind, I had never opened the book.

Daily and unashamedly, I read the New Testament. This took courage for a tough, smart aleck Marine! I don't know what the Diggers around me thought as they saw me daily reading the Bible. It didn't matter, for this was a life-and-death issue to me. Soon our outfit would leave Australia for real combat in the islands of the South Pacific. Deep in my heart I had the premonition that I would be, and deserved to be, one of the Marine casualties of war.

That's when I began to pray. I knew only two prayers: the Child's Prayer and the Lord's Prayer. I repeated them both many times each day. Jeremiah 29:13 says, *"You will seek me and find me when you seek me with all your heart."* Fortunately, God looks past the words and looks into the heart for our true motives. He knew I was searching for Him.

But I was also beginning to understand that we reap what we sow. Again Jeremiah says, *"I the Lord search the heart, and examine the mind, to reward a man according to his conduct, according to what his deeds deserve"* (Jer. 17:10).

I now realized, through my spiritually foggy mind, that what had happened to me on the streets of Ballarat was the climax of a long series of sowing and reaping. R. A. Torrey said, "It is absolutely certain that if a man sins, his own sin will dog him, that it will keep on his track night and day like a bloodhound, and never quit until it catches him and brings him to bay."

My sins were dogging me. In utter misery, I knew I needed to get right with God and find peace with Him. I couldn't go ahead in life without somehow, some way dealing with the problems of sin, sowing and reaping. *"Do not be deceived: God cannot be mocked. A man reaps what he sows"* (Gal. 6:7).

The day the cast was removed was one of the most dramatic moments of my young life. Gingerly and with great apprehension, I began to try to move my thumb. It worked . . . slowly and weakly.

For several weeks I went to an Aussie gym to strengthen my thumb and wrist. The feeling and strength slowly ebbed back and I was the happiest Marine in the First Tank Battalion. It took many weeks, but by the time of my first amphibious combat landing at Cape Gloucester, I was about full strength, although the scar was still very sensitive.

The Battle of Ballarat was the climax of the extremities in my young life. Soon after being released from the hospital, we were sent to Melbourne to await a ship to take us to the South Pacific. Daily, I continued to read the New Testament and began to experience that this is the book that understands me. I was a hungry searcher for God.

In the pages of the Gideon-issued New Testament I discovered that Jesus Christ loved me so much that He had been willing to die for all my sins: the fights, the excessive drinking, using His name in vain, and all the rest. On Goodenough Island near New Guinea, three months from the time I began reading the New Testament, I accepted Jesus Christ as my Lord and Savior. I discovered the peace of heart that transcends all human understanding.

Two years later on the island of Okinawa, when the bullet with my name on it would slam through my neck during my third combat experience, the hope of Christ's death and resurrection would sustain me in the face of death. True, I had lost the Battle of Ballarat, but I had won a spiritual war. God's undeserved favor and love enabled me to make the right turn at the crossroads in my young life.

Forty-four years later in 1987, when we lived in Australia for two years, I had the opportunity to revisit Ballarat and speak to four of the five Rotary Clubs. When I told the above story and came to the part about breaking the butcher shop window, a man named John jumped up and interrupted me saying, "That was my father's butcher shop! I was ten years old at the time!" I assured him I, by the order of my battalion commanding officer, had paid for the window and had apologized to his father.

After the meeting John and I talked, but I felt he was cool toward spiritual matters. Over the next few years I wrote him several times, but he never answered. To meet him in the Rotary Club was, to me, somewhat of a miracle.

Fifty years from the smashing of the butcher shop window, in February 1993, and six years after first meeting John at the Rotary Club, my wife and I took another trip to Ballarat during a ministry journey to Australia. We visited the mayor to thank him for the hospitality of the town to the Marines five decades ago.

I told him the story of "The Battle of Ballarat" in 1943, but that I had forgotten John's family name. Mayor James Coughlan, on his own initiative, found five family names of old-time butcher shop owners. I recognized John's name as one of them.

On a short visit to John's home, I found him broken in health at age sixty. But now his heart was open to spiritual matters. He clearly recognized that he was on the home stretch of life, thundering toward the finish line and needed God's help. It was my privilege to pray with and for John in the living room of his home. Jesus said in Matthew 18:3 that to enter the kingdom of God it is necessary for us to turn and become as little children.

In 1943 in the little town of Ballarat, God had overruled the foolishness of this young Marine who repented. God wrought the miracle of a turned life. Fifty years later through amazing circumstances, God also worked a miracle in the life of the butcher's son.

CORP. C. ASHTON   CORP. H. J. BRIDENHAGEN

The motley old breed in the making. R. Boardman, top row, center.

Sparky's wedding in Philadelphia, 1946. I'm his best man. Chapter Two.

Lt. Jerry "The Sieve" Atkinson and Cpl. Bob Boardman, Receiving Hospital, San Francisco after the battle of Okinawa, 31 July, 1945. Chapter One.

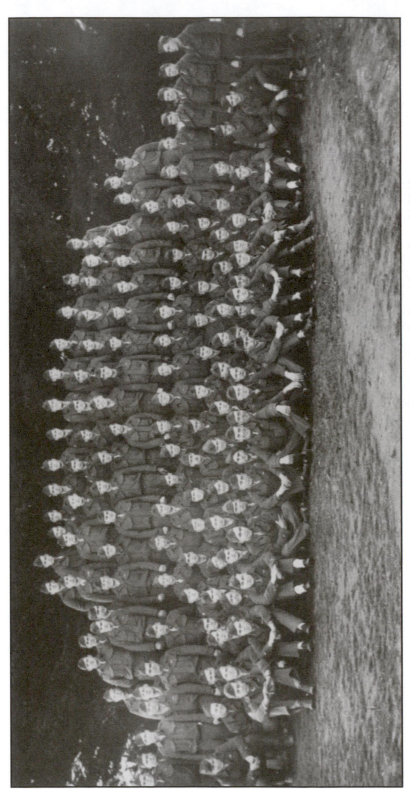

C Company, First Tank Battalion, First Marine Division, Ballarat, Australia, mid 1943.

To: My dear friends and fellow Marine Bob Boardman with warmest wishes. best God's richest blessings Mitch Paige AUSTRALIA 1943

Mitch Paige, Medal of Honor and battlefield commission to second Lieutenant, Guadalcanal, 1942, Chapter Seven.

Lt. Col. Walter "MuMu" Moore, Vietnam, commanding Second Battalion, Fifth Marine Regiment, Chapter Twenty-Four.

III. OUR FANATICAL
ENEMY

NINE

A 9,000-MILE HORSEBACK RIDE

Underestimating the Enemy

Great works are performed, not by strength, but by perseverance. He that shall walk, with vigor, three hours a day, will pass,
in seven years, a space equal to the circumference of the globe.
—*Johnson*

Yasumasa Fukushima was born into a samurai family in 1858.
"He was a veritable Don Quixote of soldiers. His courage and
his drive, his exuberant cheerfulness, were amazing. For a man
like him, nothing was impossible. Tell him something was impossible, and he would immediately prove you wrong by doing it."*

At the age of 18, right after a visit to the United States,
Fukushima was commissioned a lieutenant in the Japanese Imperial Army. He was a man with an unusual combination of tempera-
ment and personality. This combination not only made him well
liked, but also enabled him to lead men effectively. To broaden his
perspective and experience, he was sent to Mongolia when he was
21. He then became a Japanese military attaché in Peking in 1882.
Soon afterward he toured India, thus familiarizing himself with
three other key Asian nations early in his career.

Fukushima soon gained a reputation within the Imperial Army
for winning many bets involving weapons, horsemanship, and physical prowess. He couldn't turn down a dare or challenge. In 1887, at
the age of twenty-nine, he was promoted to major and appointed
military attaché in Berlin. Here he would soon be exposed to the
greatest challenge of his military career: an outrageous dare that he

---

* Richard Deacon, *Kempei Tai* (New York: Berkeley, 1983), 67.

accepted without hesitation. Upon completion of the challenge, he became one of Japan's best-known heroes.

> "In the Japanese Army, a challenge made by a foreigner was something which, even if it might appear to be bizarre and conflict with an officer's current duties, was not to be ignored. It was largely a question of prestige and honor. One day, in company with some German officers, the conversation turned to the subject of how far a horse could be ridden day after day at a certain speed. Fukushima, who was a first-rate horseman, declared that his own horse was capable of taking him all the way from Berlin to Vladivostok."*

The Germans laughed, saying that such a feat was impossible as the distance was at least nine thousand miles! "Of course, I know how far it is," said Fukushima. "What is more, I know my horse can do it. And I myself am quite equal to the task. I am in fine fettle and used to riding in mountainous terrain."*

As they were drinking, the Germans challenged Fukushima, even offering one of their own horses as a spare for the arduous trip. To their amazement, Fukushima coolly accepted their challenge, and soon received permission from his commanders to make the trip.

The Germans greatly underestimated Fukushima's capacity and commitment to a challenge. Their dare to this indomitable man set him off on a rigorous journey in 1892 at the age of thirty-four. It carried him from Germany through two continents, including the countries of Russia, Mongolia, and Manchuria. He traveled fifteen months alone on horseback, day after day through some of the most rugged terrain and worst weather in the world. What a tempting target for brigands and robbers!

Fukushima spoke many languages well, including Russian, which undoubtedly helped him successfully accomplish his trek. Even at that time in history, he and other Japanese Army officers sensed that Russia would eventually become a future enemy of Japan. There-

---

* Richard Deacon, *Kempei Tai*, 68.

fore, Fukushima's journey was not only a bold personal adventure, but served as an intelligence-gathering mission. In fact, it began his career in the intelligence branch of the Imperial Army.

One of Fukushima's heroes was Col. Fred Burnaby, a British cavalry officer. Burnaby had made a highly publicized horseback ride from the Sudan in Africa to Khiva, Russia, in 1874, eighteen years before Fukushima's journey. This was roughly 2,400 miles. Fukushima admired and thoroughly studied Burnaby's ride. It highly motivated him and prepared him for his own adventure from Berlin to Vladivostok. Surely one challenge brings about another even greater one. It is indeed important to have a pace-setting hero to follow in this life.

Upon his arrival in Vladivostok, Fukushima caught the first available ship to Yokohama, wearing the same clothes in which he had made his rugged fifteen-month trip.

> It was a bedraggled and ragged figure who eventually reached the Japanese capital, where he was duly feted and feasted for some days. The story of his ride made him a national hero. After a public reception held in his honor, he was immediately promoted to the rank of lieutenant colonel. The clothes he had worn and his riding switch were placed in a Japanese museum. *

The amazing Fukushima, who could never refuse a challenge or dare, eventually became a general staff officer. He was sent to Egypt, Turkey, Persia, Caucasia, Arabia, Burma, Siam, and Turkestan. He served as Japan's representative at the coronation of England's Edward VII. Later he became Maj. Gen. Baron Fukushima. No challenge seemed beyond the reach of this colorful, intelligent, daring man.

---

* Richard Deacon, *Kempei Tai*, 69.

TEN

A DEATH THAT LAUNCHED MILLIONS MORE

The Pre-World War II God of the Imperial Japanese Army . . . Background for Pearl Harbor

Man is certainly stark mad; he cannot make a worm, and yet he will be making gods by dozens.

—*Montaigne*

T his chapter from my first book, *A Higher Honor*, although not directly related to World War II, is included because of the history, philosophy, and mythology of the Japanese mindset. The saga of General Nogi explains in part, the background of how a noble people like the Japanese could allow themselves over a period of many years to be deluded and tricked into believing they could conquer the world through the so-called Greater East Asia Co-Prosperity Sphere. False national pride has no boundaries or restraints when rooted in this kind of myth. Japan's culpability in World War II had to be the consequence.

Gen. Baron Maresuke Nogi held a deep commitment to Emperor Meiji (1852–1912), who reigned over Japan as the 122nd sovereign. Nogi revealed his commitment by a kind of *hara-kiri* known as *junshi*, which means "following one's lord in death." His suicide, although against the law of the land, eventually became the "divine" model by which the militaristic government inspired its troops and nation, leading them into such tragedies as the war with China and World War II. Eventually, from 1937 to 1945, Japan had 2,144,507 servicemen killed and 247,299 wounded. *

However, General Nogi's story is complex and goes much deeper than the act of *junshi* because of sorrow over his earthly lord's death. Upon tracing the general's life, we find that he sought an auspicious occasion to die because of his past failures. He finally found that opportunity at the death of his emperor.

Nogi hoped that *junshi* would do three things for him and his country: first, help restore *bushido* (the way of the warrior with its traditional moral values) to Japan. Nogi recognized an increasing decadence in Japanese society. In contrast, *bushido* stressed the virtues of courage, honor, will power, and absolute loyalty to one's feudal master.

Second, Nogi desired that his act of *junshi* would show his genuine remorse and distress over the death of Emperor Meiji. Third, it would expiate the great guilt of failure that gripped him much of his life. His self-destruction, while terminating his private reality, had the potential to immortalize the prevailing myth now held by the public—that Nogi was a true samurai hero.

It is important to learn something of Nogi's background in order to more fully understand both the military code he held, and also the frustrations that began to grip his life. A strong river of circumstances seemed to sweep Maresuke Nogi along inexorably from the time of his birth in Tokyo in 1858.

The Nogis had been of samurai stock for many generations. Was there any way that this youngster could escape from this time-honored military profession? The family had grown up under the ultra-nationalistic teachings of a Chinese man named Wang Yang Ming (1492–1529), who taught that one's noble lord should be upheld even at the cost of one's life.

As a small child, Nogi was not strong. He had a delicate build, and tended to whimper and cry much of the time. In fact, one of his nicknames was Nakito, translated "Cry Baby." Perhaps he had many good reasons to cry. "One day in mid-winter when his father

---

* Theodore Ropp, "World War II": *World Book Encyclopedia*, Vol. 21 (1973), 411.

heard him complaining to his mother, he dragged him to the edge of the well, stripped him naked, and doused him with icy water."*

Nogi was born just before the close of the Tokugawa Era and "was in the last generation of Japanese samurai children fully imbued with the mystical symbol of the samurai sword. When a samurai's son passed into manhood, between ages thirteen and fifteen, he was presented with a *katana,* a long sword that he could wear along with the medium-sized *wakizashi.*

At that time in his life, there were clear indications that Nogi greatly desired to swim against the strong currents of circumstances. He felt himself unfit for a military career. As the first son of an important Choshu official, he was deeply immersed in the study of Chinese classics, poetry, archery, riflery, horsemanship, and military history.

One day, at age fourteen, Nogi requested of his father that he be allowed to become a scholar instead of a samurai bureaucrat. As he expected, his father categorically refused. Japan's history, yes, even world history, might have been different had Nogi been allowed to become a scholar. But the currents were too strong, especially for the first son in the family.

Nogi's younger brother, Makoto, was larger, stronger, and a more natural candidate for the tough disciplines of a samurai, but fate had made her decision in favor of the oldest son. The lives of thousands, even millions of young men would later be needlessly squandered as General Nogi clung to antiquated, prideful traditions over wisdom and common sense.

It is difficult to tell at this point in history, but perhaps a light in the soul of Nogi was then extinguished, never to be rekindled again, when his father, a martial arts expert, made the decision that Nogi was to follow the samurai tradition and not the path of a scholar. How many other young careers have been decided in like manner by inflexible, authoritarian elders, only to add eventually to the deep woes of an already over-burdened world?

---

* "General Nogi: The Pre-War God of the Army," *The East.* (June–July, 1968), 6.
† R. J. Lifton and S. Kato, *Six Lives, Six Deaths* (New Haven: Yale UP, 1979), 36.

Upon his father's refusal to allow him to become a scholar, Nogi left home and found refuge in the nearby home of a relative, Bunnoshin Tamaki. Tamaki, along with one of his zealous disciples, began to teach Nogi ideological lessons.

This ideology "combined emperor-centered nationalism and samurai self-discipline with a pragmatic awareness of the superiority of Western technology."*

A short time later, the 250-year-old Tokugawa shogunate collapsed and the party of antishogun samurai set up a new government. All this was done bloodlessly in the name of young Emperor Meiji; therefore, it is known as the Meiji Restoration.

Through all of these upheavals, there emerged ideological and loyalty struggles between Nogi's samurai roots in Kyushu and the fledgling Meiji government. In these struggles and shifting loyalties, Nogi's brother, Makoto, was killed in a revolt in Kyushu. At the same time, Tamaki, Nogi's former mentor, committed suicide when he realized that the revolt had failed. The Meiji government formed the Japanese Imperial Army, and Nogi, at the age of twenty-two, was appointed a major. Although loyal to the emperor, Nogi experienced great stress because he was caught between his Kyushu roots and the order to lead government troops against the revolution.

In 1877, while in command of a government regiment, Nogi made a reckless frontal assault against Kumamoto Castle in Kyushu. During fierce fighting, the regimental flag bearer was killed and the flag was lost to the rebels. This flag had been presented by Emperor Meiji to the regiment and was regarded by many, including Nogi, as a sacred object.

Nogi, under great guilt, wanted to personally search for the flag, and had to be physically restrained. Such an act would have meant certain death. While some superiors advocated drastic punishment for Nogi, he was finally let off with only a reprimand. However, the disgrace of losing the regimental flag remained with Nogi until the day of his *junshi*. In his ten-point last will and testament, point number one centered on this incident:

---

* R. J. Lifton and S. Kato, *Six Lives, Six Deaths,* 39.

On this occasion of the passing of Emperor Meiji, I am filled with remorse and have decided to commit suicide. I am aware of the gravity of this crime. Nevertheless, since I lost the regimental colors in the battle of 1877, I have searched in vain for an opportunity to die. To this day I have been treated with unmerited kindness, receiving abundant imperial favors. Gradually, I have become old and weak; my time has disappeared and I can no longer serve my lord. Feeling extremely distressed by his death, I have resolved to end my life. *

Wherever Nogi went throughout his tragic career, failure and death seemed to follow. Even so, there would always be some kind of amazing cover-up, and then he would personally partially recover. Nevertheless, he lived under a great guilt complex all of his life, as revealed partially in this brief portion of his will. Three times he was suspended from the military, and three times he was recalled for further responsibilities. During each of his suspensions, he withdrew to a farm plot he had purchased in Tochigi Prefecture.

It has been aptly pointed out that in Nogi's withdrawal from society, he adhered to two important Japanese cultural principles: Avoid direct confrontation within the group through passive rather than active protest—and assume the role of the wise hermit.

Following his first suspension, he was recalled and promoted in December 1892 to be commander of the First Infantry Brigade in Tokyo. During the Sino-Japanese War of 1894–1895, he was victorious in many battles in China. Nogi's troops captured Port Arthur on the tip of the Liao-Dong Peninsula in southern Manchuria in one day from the Chinese. He was then promoted to the rank of lieutenant general. His unit proceeded to Taiwan in late 1895 to help "liberate" the island by combating a resistance movement. Soon Nogi was appointed governor of Taiwan, but he was unsuccessful in that position because he was unable to handle complex colonial problems using his moralistic samurai theories. This led to his second suspension.

---

* R. J. Lifton and S. Kato, *Six Lives, Six Deaths*, 31.

The outbreak of the Russo-Japanese War in 1904 brought Nogi's recall to active duty once again. He was appointed commanding officer of the Third Japanese Imperial Army and was again ordered to capture Port Arthur, now held and especially well fortified by the Russians. Perhaps his superiors, and Nogi himself, felt that because of his previous victory against the Chinese, the port city would be a walkover. But such was not the case. Here began one of the greatest and most useless carnages in Japanese military history. It was perpetuated by a proud but incompetent general clinging to outmoded means of warfare.

Nogi's "strategy" was simply an all-out frontal attack. In the first assault during August, the cream of Japan's youth met Russian machine guns blazing from the uphill fortress. Fifteen thousand men were killed. That was almost one-third of the 50,700 troops under Nogi's command

Nogi then waited until October and ordered a second frontal assault that failed, and then in November a third head-on attack, which was also futile. The uphill assault path was soaked and resoaked a crimson color. Littered among the dead, the wounded, and dying repeatedly called out, *"Okasan, okasan!"*—"Mother, mother!" But there were no loving mothers to answer. Soon these pitiful words emerging from horribly mangled bodies turned to a cacophony of helpless, dying moans.

Imperial headquarters had originally favored the capture of adjacent Hill Meter 203, instead of the deadly frontal assault. Nogi was adamantly against this tactic, but now, with his repeated failures, he finally turned his surviving troops toward Hill 203. Thirteen thousand more young men died taking 203. A total of 240 nightmarish days were spent in the siege of Port Arthur before it finally fell. "Nogi's relentless, bloody and futile assaults throughout the autumn of 1904 cost 56,000 Japanese casualties, sacrifices for which he felt personally responsible."*

A British reporter who was at the scene gave the following graphic witness of the siege of Port Arthur:

---

* Mark R. Pearle, "Nogi Maresuke," *Kodansha Encyclopedia of Japan,* Vol. 6, (1983), 31.

The horrors of the struggle seem to belong rather to a barbaric age than to the twentieth century. The miserable fate of thousands of wounded, who, had they been attended to, would have been saved, will ever form a dark page in warfare. The struggle was rendered intensely interesting by the fact that the Japanese endeavored to combine modern weapons and methods of destruction with obsolete formations in attack. The result was unprecedented carnage: and we have probably witnessed these old-fashioned assaults on forts for the last time. *

General Nogi not only lost his honor and face and became a military disgrace because of his tragic and senseless leadership, but both of his sons also died at Port Arthur, leaving him without a male heir. His oldest son was killed just before Nogi left Japan for China. His second son was one of the victims of his father's futile frontal assaults on the fortress.

At Port Arthur, Nogi was quietly relieved of command of the attack by Gen. Gentaro Kodama, General Chief of Staff. Kodama reopened the assault and within one week was victorious.

For a time Japan's press and public condemned Nogi as the butcher of Port Arthur, but history is a fickle master. The eventual triumph of Japan over Russia in the war helped to restore Nogi's public image. Japan, a tiny nation, was the first Asian country to defeat a Western nation in modern warfare—and that nation was geographically the largest in the world! This was indeed a heady victory.

Nogi, the failure, became a hero. He was decorated by Prussia, Romania, Great Britain, France, and Chile. He also visited many foreign countries as an official state representative of the Japanese government. He became a worldwide symbol of the Japanese fearless warrior. Yet in his inner being, Nogi thought of himself as a failure and was filled with despair. He continued to be preoccupied with his own death, and searched for an opportune time to end his life.

---

* R. J. Lifton and S. Kato, *Six Lives, Six Deaths*, 52.

His day of atonement came on September 13, 1912, the day the imperial funeral of Emperor Meiji began. The period of mourning for the emperor was fifty-six days. During that period it is recorded that General Nogi visited the palace 156 times. His fidelity to the emperor was unquestioned.

It is evident that Nogi did not plan for his wife, Shizuko, to die with him. In his will, written the night before Emperor Meiji's funeral, she was the chief beneficiary. She, however, chose to follow her husband's course of death when she realized that he planned to commit *junshi*. That fateful morning, Nogi and Shizuko had their pictures taken in formal dress. Then she wrote the following sad, thirty-one-syllable *tanka*:

> "I go, never to return,
> Regretting only the passing of today's joy."

Nogi had to help Shizuko with her *junshi* because she was too weak to complete it. He then proceeded to perform his own *junshi*. Nogi's last tanka poem said:

> My Lord has gone to heaven,
> I humbly follow after. *

After his death, Nogi's life became increasingly held in mythical proportions, until eventually he was worshipped as a god. In the heart of Tokyo there is a Shinto shrine in his honor, but today hardly anyone ever visits it. Nogi remains, however, a unique character in Japanese history.

> Alive, Nogi destroyed the lives of many Japanese and Russians; dead, his legacy, as a symbolic tool of Japanese militarism, helped to destroy the lives of many more Japanese, as well as Chinese and Americans. He created nothing. *

---

* "General Nogi," *The East,* 10.
† R. J. Lifton and S. Kato, *Six Lives, Six Deaths,* 62.

We Are Responsible for the Decisions We Make

What lessons can we learn from this tragic figure, who seemed so helplessly trapped in the onward flow of the river of circumstances? The English poet Lord Byron said, *"Men are the sport of circumstances, when the circumstances seem the sport of men."*

If we allow our lives to be carried along by fate and circumstances, then we hold to a fatalistic view of life. It is the belief that nothing or no one can change our direction or the meaning of life. If we follow this existential outlook, then only tragedy and wild guesswork await us on the path of life. Our future can only be as grim as Nogi's and his wife's. Even though their pathway was fatalistic, their samurai training allowed them in the end to stoically compose a farewell *tanka*. That is more than most existentialists can do when their time to die approaches.

Many people are carried along by the current of overwhelming circumstances. Life becomes a trap, and although the end may not be as dramatic as Nogi's, it is nevertheless just as grim. Some people hope that, while facing the challenge of death, it will suffice for them to muster the aesthetic stoicism to compose a farewell poem. But it is not enough.

There is a point of no return in this life, and somewhere along the line, Nogi passed it. From that time on, many of his decisions were calamities that led to increased failure and frustration—and ultimately to tragic death by his own hand.

Today we cannot say for sure at what point Nogi arrived at the crossroads of life when he should have taken a different path. Somewhere along the road he could have chosen the right way, even though the price would probably have been enormous. It might have cost him all he had—yes, even his life as a young man.

Scripture speaks plainly of the Crossroads of Life where a person faces the importance of making good and right decisions. It speaks of wisdom, common sense, and understanding:

Does not wisdom call and discernment utter her voice? On the top of the heights along the way, at the crossroads she takes her stand; beside the gates, in front of the town, from the portals' entrance she cries out: "To you, O men, I call; my voice is directed to the sons of men. O simple ones, learn to get insight. O fools, Make your mind understand." (Prov. 8:1–6 TBV).

Although the circumstances of your life may seem overwhelming, you are responsible to make good and just decisions. You can move toward the right road, even if, in the past, you chose the wrong way at the crossroads. Stop—listen—turn back—repent—call out to the living God who controls all circumstances and loves you.

He is the God who is sovereign over the whole earth. He longs to be sovereign over your life through faith in His Son, Jesus Christ. He wants to guide you away from the path of no return.

ELEVEN

HIDDEN IN THE JUNGLE FOR TWENTY-EIGHT YEARS

Fanatical Dedication and Perseverance

Nothing in the world can take the place of persistence. Talent will not; nothing is more common than unsuccessful men with talent. Genius will not; unrewarded genius is almost a proverb. Education will not; the world is full of educated derelicts. Persistence and determination alone are omnipotent.

—Calvin Coolidge

Shoichi Yokoi was one of the few Japanese soldiers who survived the US Marine invasion of Guam in 1944. He not only lived through the invasion, but he also lived on successfully evading capture in the jungles for twenty-eight more years. He might still be there if he hadn't been discovered by two Guamanians one day while he was fishing.

A private in the Imperial Japanese Army, Yokoi had been transferred to Guam from Manchuria in March 1944. The Japanese had captured Guam from the Americans the same day they had attacked Pearl Harbor. Now, in mid-1944, the fortunes of war had turned. Within four months of Yokoi's arrival, the US Marines made their amphibious invasion of the island on July 21, rapidly moving inland. Yokoi's outfit was decimated. He and seven comrades fled into the jungle in an attempt to survive.

Guam is one of the most conducive islands for sustaining man's efforts to survive. Its year-round temperature seldom varies from a range of seventy to seventy-nine degrees Fahrenheit. Edible fruits abound. There are no poisonous snakes or dangerous animals. Thirty miles long and four to eight miles wide, the island is the largest of the many in the Mariana Group, giving the soldiers plenty of room to hide.

Yokoi and his seven cohorts began their desperate fight for survival deep in the recesses of the northern jungles. By 1946 only three were alive. Then until 1960, Yokoi and his two younger compatriots shared the same cave. But after fourteen years together, with opinions and tempers clashing, the inevitable split came and the two younger men moved to another cave five hundred yards away. Nevertheless, because they had gone through the hardships of combat and jungle survival together, the three were still comrades.

> On New Year's Day 1964, Mr. Yokoi went to visit his friends. When he reached their cave, he called their names. Hearing no reply, he entered the cave and found them dead, their bodies having already been reduced to skeletons. At that moment he had a strong urge to die, but he persevered. *

For eight more years Yokoi was completely alone in the jungle. He kept mice, wild chickens, birds, and a caged toad as pets to help stave off loneliness. He became a master at avoiding detection, although he was almost discovered by Guamanians several times. His normal routine was to leave his cave only at sunset to search for food, and then he selected only a few coconuts and wild plants to avoid discovery. He was extremely careful to cover his footprints in the soft soil or sand. Daily he encountered wild bees, mites, mosquitoes, leeches, cockroaches, lizards, and non-poisonous snakes.

Yokoi became his own doctor and pharmacist, creating cave-brewed medicines to ward off infection from cuts, scratches, and bites. Using his steel helmet, he would brew up concoctions made from toad fat, toad livers, river eels, and burnt, unripe coconuts in

---

* "Wisdom from Life in the Guamanian Jungle," *The East* (May 1984), 10.

order to ward off diarrhea and stomach cramps. This inventive jungle survivor always boiled his drinking water, even though it came from a well in a corner of his cave and appeared to be safe.

Knowing that greens were essential for his health, he watched what plants the deer ate, then ate the same kinds. He always boiled them first. His essential protein came from toads and wild mice cooked tempura style in coconut oil. As a careful nutritionist, he decided that he would stop eating when his stomach was half full, believing that this was essential for good health.

Yokoi's genius for survival was revealed in other ways as well. Through the years he fashioned a type of flush toilet in his cave, utilizing the rainwater that seeped into the cave. He dug a drainage ditch that passed under his toilet carrying the sewage down to a stream below the cave. Years later, "an engineering designer of Takenaka Komuten Company was quite impressed by Yokoi's cave dwelling. He wondered how Yokoi managed to do the drainage work without a design drawing."*

Repeatedly in Yokoi's saga of survival, we see the truth that necessity is indeed the mother of invention. This was particularly true in how he made his clothing. Before being drafted into the army, Yokoi had been a professional tailor. Since his army uniform was entirely worn out by 1950, six years after he plunged into his rugged jungle environment, he needed some new protection from the swarms of mosquitoes and the heavy underbrush of the jungle.

Discovering that strips from the hibiscus tree could be made into thread, Yokoi, with childhood memories of his mother working at a loom, fashioned a primitive loom and went to work. It took three months to weave enough material for one long sleeve shirt and a pair of trousers. After the jungle survivor returned to Japan, a Chinese tailor, impressed with Yokoi's unique skills, offered him employment at an extremely high wage. Here is a description of his jungle clothing:

> The shirt had five buttons and a collar, and the cuffs of
> the pants narrowed around the ankle and were secured

---

* "Wisdom from Life in the Guamanian Jungle," *The East* (May 1984), 19.

with buttons so as to allow easy movement in the jungle. The buttons were made of pieces of coconut shell, which were ground into the round shape using a stone, and were pierced with a red-hot wire to make a hole. The button-holes were carefully reinforced with a string. The needles he used were made from pieces of cannon shells. He tailored three shirts, three pair of pants, a vest, a pair of knee pants during his life in the jungle. Mr. Yokoi spent half a year making just one shirt and a pair of pants. He recalls that "it was hard work, but I was always encouraged by the joy of creation."*

One day as he was deep in the jungle preoccupied with catching shrimp, two Guamanians sneaked up on him. The indomitable survivor snatched one of their pistols and tried to escape. But the men grabbed him, pinned him to the ground, bound his hands together, and then led him to their home where they fed him. Though Yokoi was suffering from malnutrition, the men testified that "his steps were sure and he was quite articulate."

On January 24, 1972, Yokoi's twenty-eight-year reclusive ordeal finally ended. The outside world was astounded to hear that this Japanese soldier had held out for nearly three decades without surrendering. But to the Japanese of Yokoi's generation, it was no mystery. Part of Imperial Japan's teaching was that it was a disgrace to surrender in battle. To die in battle for the emperor was a high privilege. Furthermore, it had been drilled into the Japanese soldiers that they would be tortured to death if captured. Thus, when Yokoi received care and hospitality from the Guamanians, he was utterly amazed. His fears were replaced by thanksgiving.

In early February 1972, Yokoi arrived back in Japan, his homeland which, in his persevering way, he had been attempting to serve by remaining uncaptured in the jungles. At Tokyo's Haneda International Airport the fifty-six-year-old survivor made the following statement, revealing his shame upon returning to his homeland

---

* "Wisdom from Life in the Guamanian Jungle," *The East* (May 1984), 20.

without giving up his life for his country: "I, Shoichi Yokoi, have survived and come back despite my great shame"*

Yokoi viewed with utter incredulity and interest both the technological and sociological changes that had taken place in Japan. He issued this message to his people: "Today's children lack the experience of hardship. Parents spoil their children, who, in turn, take parental love for granted."†

Although Yokoi could easily have capitalized on his ordeal, he deliberately chose a simple lifestyle. He wrote a book entitled *Live a Tougher Life,* extolling the simple lifestyle. Now married, he quietly cultivates his own vegetable garden and produces pottery in his own kiln.

Living a Tougher Life

People in general, and Christians in particular, can learn much from this modern-day Robinson Crusoe. His perseverance and creativity in the midst of personal suffering bought out the kind of potential that lies deep within all of us. We need not give up when faced with any kind of hardship, great or small. The commitment of this non-Christian never to give up should challenge Christians, who often tend to forget the importance of perseverance.

St. Paul admonished the Corinthians by his own example of perseverance in the midst of intense suffering when he said, *"I am . . . always getting a knockdown, but never a knock-out . . . So I never give up"* (2 Cor. 4:8–9, 16 WNT).

The apostle's greatest creativity in his God-inspired writings came out of a lifetime of suffering for the gospel. Trials will bring out the best in us if we trust. It is much like the painful procedure of heating and reheating metal to remove the dross in order to make it pure and pliable.

Suffering produces perseverance (Rom. 5:3–4). If we want to be more steadfast, there are no shortcuts. Why is it that we today, especially in developed countries, lack the kind of insight into the illusion of material gain that Yokoi had? Why don't we also make

---

* "Wisdom from Life in the Guamanian Jungle," *The East* (May 1984), 18.
† Ibid, 20.

the deliberate choice of simplicity? Scripture gives us clear guidelines for the right perspective on material things:

> There is great gain in godliness with contentment; for we brought nothing into the world, and we cannot take anything out of the world; but if we have food and clothing, with these we shall be content. But those who desire to be rich fall into temptation, into a snare, into many senseless and hurtful desires that plunge men into ruin and destruction. (1 TIM. 6:6–9 RSV)

Many in Yokoi's position would be bitter after his experience. Didn't he lose twenty-eight years of his life? Didn't "life pass him by?" Think of all the historical events and material gain he missed.

Yet this unforgettable man received a tranquility of soul in the seclusion of the jungle. He gained invaluable advantages precisely because he missed all the things that so many of us cling to, things that fade away as mist that arises and then disappears forever. The writer of Ecclesiastes sums up the whole matter very well: *"Better is a handful with quietness than both hands full, together with toil and grasping for the wind"* (Eccles. 4:6 NKJV).

When we become sidetracked in life by material gain, we lose our tranquility of soul. Yokoi's experience points us in a direction that we should ardently pursue: *"Better is a little with the fear of the Lord, than great treasure with trouble. Better is a dinner of herbs where love is, than a fatted calf with hatred"* (Prov. 5:16–17, NKJV).

TWELVE

THE ULTIMATE APOLOGY

Is Suicide the Answer?

Death is the great adventure beside which moon landings and
space trips pale into insignificance.

—*Joseph Bayly*

I sao Matsuo, Flying Petty Officer First Class, wrote in his last
letter to his parents before his Kamikaze mission,

> Please congratulate me. I have been given a splendid opportu-
> nity to die. This is my last day. How I appreciate this chance to
> die like a man. Thank you, parents, for the 23 years during which
> you have cared for me and inspired me. Cherry blossoms glisten
> as they open and fall . . . I shall fall like a blossom from a radiant
> cherry tree. *

A Japanese sergeant in the Palau Islands led his men into battle
singing a line from an old war song, "He will fall like a blossom in
war."[†]

The blossoms these men write about come from an old Japanese poem:

Like cherry blossoms
In the spring,

---

* Capt. Rikihei Inoguchi and Comdr. Tadashi Nakajima, with Roger Pineau,
The Divine Wind (Bantam Books: New York, 1958), 178-9.

[†] Hiroshi Funasaka, *Falling Blossoms* (Times Books International: Singapore,
1986), p. 5.

Let us fall
Clean and radiant. *

The falling blossoms are soldiers dying in warfare.

Ensign Heiichi Okabe, a twenty-two-year-old university graduate, kept a diary as he prepared for his suicide mission. He wrote, "What is the duty today? It is to fight. What is the duty tomorrow? It is to win. What is the daily duty? It is to die. My life will be rounded out in the next thirty days. My chance will come. Death and I are waiting. We die in battle without complaint."[†] And die they did. Japan recorded over 2,144,507 servicemen killed and over 247,299 wounded in World War II fighting.[‡]

Though soldiers from both sides died bravely for their country in World War II, the Japanese had a totally different view of death. They welcomed it. US Navy Vice Adm. C. R. Brown said,

> One of the earliest lessons one learns in battle is that courage is a very common quality. But there was a fundamental difference in the heroism of the opposing warrior. The Japanese resolutely closed the last avenue of hope and escape, the American never did. No one has yet successfully explained to the Western mind his Japanese phenomenon of self-immolation, and perhaps it is not given to the Westerner to understand it.[§]

This Japanese attitude toward death can only be partially fathomed by understanding the *Hagakure,* the classic book of samurai ethics and behavior. The single most often quoted line of the *Hagakure* is, "I have discovered that the Way of the Samurai is death," a phrase which became the slogan to spur on young kami-

---

* Hiroshi Funasaka, *Falling Blossoms* (Times Books International: Singapore, 1986), p. 5.
† Hiroshi Funasaka, *Falling Blossoms* (Times Books International: Singapore, 1986), p. 5.
‡ Theodore Ropp, "World War II": *World Book Encyclopedia,* Vol. 21 (1973), p. 411.
§ Capt. Rikihei Inoguchi and Comdr. Tadashi Nakajima, with Roger Pineau, *The Divine Wind* (Bantam Books: New York, 1958), 185.

kaze pilots. The *Hagakure* goes on to say, "In a fifty-fifty life or death crisis, simply settle it by choosing immediate death. One who chooses to go on living having failed in one's mission will be despised as a coward and a bungler . . . in order to be a perfect samurai, it is necessary to prepare oneself for death morning and evening, day in and day out."[*]

Yukio Mishima, a Japanese novelist who himself committed ceremonial hara-kiri in 1970, wrote:

> *Hagakure* is based on the principles of the samurai. The occupation of the samurai is death. No matter how peaceful the age, death is the samurai's supreme motivation, and if a samurai should fear or shun death, in that instant he would cease to be a samurai.[†]

This attitude toward death enabled the Japanese army to use a variety of "suicide" attacks in warfare. The method used by the Kamikaze pilots, who smashed into our ships, is perhaps the best known. There is the *banzai* attack, a word now listed in our English dictionary as "reckless, suicidal." Another method was called the "living bomb" in which the Japanese soldier would hold an explosive charge and allow himself to be crushed beneath the treads of an oncoming tank. And yet another was called the "obstruction strategy," where their soldiers would dive to their death into the tank's treads, thus immobilizing the tank until the mangled body could be removed.

Our military men daily faced this indomitable samurai spirit in the Pacific Theater, a spirit which made the Japanese such an intrepid enemy. And, naturally, not all of the Japanese soldiers wanted to die. On Okinawa, several thousand surrendered when they saw that the war was lost. Some hesitated only because their leaders said the Americans would kill them, but surrender they did.

---

[*] Yukio Mishima, *The Way of the Samurai* (The Putnam Publishing Group: New York, 1977), vii.

[†] Yukio Mishima, *The Way of the Samurai*, 27.

The Ultimate Apology

The Western world rejects the samurai's emphasis on learning how to die before learning how to live. We call this type of training a misguided tragedy. Why should a youth of fifteen learn how to die when he has not yet tasted the joy of living? Why does any man need to be trained to take his own life when it is so important to stay alive?

Westerners understand the justice and honor of fighting and dying for a cause, but to believe that *hara-kiri* (*hara* means "belly," *kiri* means "cut"), or stomach cutting, is an honorable death is difficult, if not impossible, for us to accept.

It was believed in the days of the samurai that the real person (the soul and all the qualities of courage) dwelt in the stomach or bowels. Currently the Japanese language includes nearly seventy idiomatic expressions containing the word *hara* (also pronounced *fuku*).

To open the stomach is to reveal everything to everyone. It is to say, by one supreme act, here is my heart, courage, and sincerity—my true self. I can give no more. Please forgive me. Accept this ultimate apology as a cleansing of my good name.

During World War II, countless Japanese soldiers, especially officers, committed suicide in the Pacific. Immediately following the surrender in 1945, ultra-patriotic men and women committed *hara-kiri* on the Imperial Palace grounds as an apology to the emperor for having lost the war. It is truly the ultimate apology.

IV. PELELIU . . . ISLAND
OF JUDGMENT

AUTHOR'S INTRODUCTION
TO PELELIU
Some Thoughts on Death and Dying

For three of their four battles in World War II, the First Marine Division Reinforced was awarded the Presidential Unit Citation. Superb leadership at all levels, unquestioned courage that conquered fear, and commitment to victory over a fanatical enemy were some of the marks of this outstanding cadre of men. I count it a great privilege to have been a small part of this highly decorated and motivated division.

Death and dying are subjects that every man in a combat unit thinks deeply about. Gen. George Patton, US Army, in a speech to his troops before the Normandy invasion, gives clues on the process of conquering the fear of death. Patton and Marine Gen. Chesty Puller were cousins. Chesty always claimed that Patton should have been a Marine!

Here are Patton's words:

> Death must not be feared. Death in time comes to all of us. And every man is scared in his first action. If he says he's not, he's a liar . . . The real hero is the man who fights even though he's scared. Some get over their fright in a minute under fire.
>
> Others take an hour. For some it takes days, but a real man will never let the fear of death overpower his honor, his sense of duty to his country, or his manhood.

Gen. John A Lejeune, thirteenth Commandant of the Marine Corps, combat leader, scholar, thinker, educator, and innovator, thought deeply about life and death in battle. Some know him as "the man who charted the course of the Corps in the twentieth century." Here are some of his profound thoughts on death and dying:

> In war, if a man is to keep his sanity, he must come to regard death as being just as normal as life and hold himself always in readiness, mentally and spiritually, to answer the call of the Grim Reaper whenever fate decrees that his hour has struck.
>
> It is only by means of this state of mind and soul that a man can devote all his thoughts, all his intellect, and all his will to the execution of the task confided to him. Personal fear paralyzes all the faculties, and the attributes of first importance in a commander is freedom from its cold and clammy clutch.
>
> There is no substitute for the spiritual in war. Miracles must be wrought if victories are to be won. To work miracles, men's hearts must need be alive with self-sacrificing love for each other, for their units, for their division, and for their country.
>
> If each man knows that all the officers and men in his division are animated with the same fiery zeal as he himself feels, unquenchable courage and unconquerable determination crush out fear, and death becomes preferable to defeat or dishonor.
> —*from The Reminiscences of a Marine by Maj. Gen. John A. Lejeune (Dorrance & Co., 1930), 307, 321.*

As we approached the formidable islands of Peleliu and Okinawa—or any other battle throughout the Pacific—many of our comrades had an appointment with death. Only God knew which of our names would be called in the final muster. Each man silently and inwardly prepared himself as well as he could. Some had no premonition; others knew their name would be called.

The little known, far-off islands of Peleliu and Okinawa would bring to a violent close the lives of some of America's finest young warriors.

I Have a Rendezvous with Death

(Alan Seeger, American volunteer, age twenty-eight, killed in France while serving with the French Foreign Legion, 1916).

I have a rendezvous with Death
At some disputed barricade,
When Spring comes back with rustling shade
And apple blossoms fill the air—
I have a rendezvous with Death
When Spring brings back blue days and fair.

It may be he shall take my hand,
And lead me into his dark land,
And close my eyes and quench my breath –
It may be I shall pass him still.
I have a rendezvous with Death
On some scarred slope of battered hill,
When Spring comes round again this year
And the first meadow flowers appear.

God knows 'twere better to be deep,
Pillowed in silk and scented down,
Where Love throbs out in blissful sleep,
Pulse nigh to pulse, and breath to breath,
Where hushed awakenings are dear . . .
But I've a rendezvous with Death
At midnight in some flaming town,
When Spring trips north again this year;
And I to my pledged word am true,
I shall not fail that rendezvous.

THIRTEEN

CAPE GLOUCESTER, NEW BRITAIN

Endure Hardships as a Good Marine

Adversities do not make a man frail. They show what sort of man he is.

—*Thomas A. Kempis*

The four months the men of the First Marine Division spent on Cape Gloucester was, apart from casualties, the most rugged living and fighting conditions of any of the division's four campaigns in the Pacific—the others being Guadalcanal, Peleliu, and Okinawa. In Bernard Nulty's fine monograph he called New Britain "The Green Inferno."

The adversities couldn't be put any better than George McMillan, author of the *Old Breed*, put it:

The natural hazards of the battlefield must never equal the hazards contrived by the enemy. Break this law, put a fighting man down in a spot where the plant and animal life or the climate are as much or more of a menace to his existence than the armed human opposite him, and the fighting man will feel he is the victim of an injustice. That is why the men who fought in Cape Gloucester remember the place more for the jungle than for the Japanese. "In the next war," a sergeant said as his transport pulled away from New Britain at the end of that battle, "I ain't ever gonna plant a victory garden." *

* George McMillian, *The Old Breed* (Washington: Infantry Journal Press, 1949), 175.

New Britain is a volcanic island just off the eastern coast of New Guinea. Rabaul, its major strategic fortress base at the northwestern tip of the island, was seized by the Japanese from the Australians on 23 January 1942, near the end of the battle of Guadalcanal. Little did the Marines of the First Division on Guadalcanal realize that they would return to that part of the Southwest Pacific a few months later to land at the far end of New Britain from Rabaul and have a key part in neutralizing that great military bastion.

Several hundred thousand Japanese soldiers, sailors and airmen passed through Rabaul reinforcing their troops in New Guinea and the Solomon Islands. The airfield on Cape Gloucester was, likewise, strategic for the Japanese conquest of that part of the world. When we seized Cape Gloucester, 500 miles from Rabaul, on the same island, the Japanese could not reinforce or resupply their troops overland because of the rugged mountainous jungle terrain. There was no road and even the foot trails often completely disappeared.

During the Marines' four-month campaign, the Japanese could only attempt, sometimes in the early stages successfully, to reinforce and resupply by small boats and barges. That method did not last long once we controlled the sea and air and a good part of the coastline from Cape Gloucester to Cape Hoskins.

What goes through the mind of a Marine about to make an amphibious landing on a completely unknown, strange island shore and with a wily, tenacious enemy waiting, eager to take his life? In this case it was New Britain, but it could have been any landing or battlefield in World War II.

George McMillan gives this vivid word picture—It was the day after Christmas, 1943:

Each minute from daybreak to H-hour is a mute juror of fortitude. To each minute every man who is going into the unknown shore must make separate inward testimony. "Yes, this is me," every man must say. "It is I. This is December 1943. This is New Britain. I am on a ship. I will soon pick up this pack and rifle. I will go into a small boat. I will go to that shore. I will step out on it. I will do that. Not somebody else. Me." Such is the testimony each man must make. No other jury sits: only the sluggish minutes. Only time will decide. This internal debate seems endless, nor is there relief from it in externals. A man begins to think of himself as a spectator, finds himself looking upon all the confusion, all the noises, all the sweat and strain, including his own, all the comings and goings around him, as something outside himself. It is as if he were holding a peopled kaleidoscope in front of his eye. It is as if a series of vivid tableaux were being enacted in front of him. *

I was in C Company, First Tank Battalion, First Marine Division. We landed on Gloucester with light tanks—M5s, weighing fifteen tons. A and B Companies were equipped with the new M4A2 General Shermans weighing twice as much. Conditions on New Britain—the terrain, rain forest, swamps, the constant rain, impassable dirt roads—limited our use of tanks and other motorized vehicles. Even with those debilitating conditions tanks did an excellent task in supporting the infantry.

Many of us were fresh, green replacements into the division in Australia, plus a preponderance of veterans from Guadalcanal. We were eager to prove ourselves, although some of the veterans disdained us and did not treat us well—like poorly paid rookies in the NFL. That was ok, though difficult for us at the time. The discipline was good for us. Cape Gloucester was our proving ground.

New Britain was clearly the toughest living conditions of our two years and three campaigns in the Pacific. Memories flood back of water-filled foxholes and jungle hammocks which were a severe test of patience to string and then learn how to get into! They often filled with water, too. In time we learned that the rainwater would gradually warm up to body temperature and we could sleep on, though fitfully.

---

* George McMillian, *The Old Breed*, 172-3.

Nearly every night, we underwent bombings from a string of "Washing Machine Charlies" coming down from Rabaul. To us, their engines sounded like mom's Maytag washing machine back home. These bombings were harassments designed to keep the division awake—and, of course, to do some damage. One Charlie would finish his run and then another would take his place through the whole night.

We learned over time to stay in our hammocks until the last possible moment. When we heard the bombs whistle as they fell, we would roll out and dash for our nearby foxhole. Every so often a Marine's hammock zipper would get stuck in the mosquito netting—panic all the way—and afterwards, very comical. He took the brunt of our jokes. Falling bombs are a terrifying experience. Lots of confusion, exhaustion, and, of course, some casualties.

All tankers salute the heart of the First Marine Division and of any division, the mud-Marines or infantry, the First, Fifth, and Seventh Regiments. After the intense battle for Hill 660, the Seventh Marines had survived twenty-three straight days in the rain forest fighting until relieved by the Fifth:

> It was raining the day they scrambled back down [Hill 660] and one observer noted that "wetness is now as much a part of them as the clayish mud that blends helmets and boots, into the reddish-brown of the soil. Some are slopped over with ochre-stained ponchos, some hooded by Japanese raincoats. They eat as they trudge along, cold beans and cold hash out of cans." And already many had begun to come down with malaria. Even the dead suffered from the rain. In the new graveyard at the airfield the sharply spaded mounds that marked each bier were eroded and leveled by rain and each morning it was necessary for the men who kept the cemetery to go out with shovels and rebuild the mounds. It rained on January 19, the day the cemetery was dedicated . . . *

The Japanese troops suffered even more than the Marines in the inhumane condition of the eastern end of New Britain. Many

---

* George McMillian, *The Old Breed*, 206.

of their units were isolated from each other. Their reinforcements and supplies dwindled and eventually stopped altogether. Toward the end of the campaign some Japanese were not only under-nourished and hungry but also in advanced stages of starvation. All of this made them increasingly vulnerable to foot rot, ma-laria, skin disease and dysentery. When our patrols came across emaciated enemy too weak to fight or walk, these Japanese often blew themselves up with the single hand-grenade allotted to them for that purpose.

Lots of praying goes on before and during any battle—and of-ten it slacks off afterwards, for *man's extremity is God's opportunity*. Here are the profound thoughts of a Marine in the Seventh Regi-ment after a Japanese sniper tied in the top of a tree had shot his close buddy near Hill 660:

> I began to pray. I lost my rosary, but I had a Holy Family medal. I prayed most of the time, I guess, except when I was *thinking*. When I got to thinking then I had the loneli-est feeling I ever had in my life. There'd be a million guys around and you'd still feel lonely. Sometimes when we were pinned down, waiting to try again, I'd lay there with my face as deep in the ground as I could get it. And I'd fix my eyes on something. Once it was an ant. Once it was just a blade of grass . . . I was in a daze . . . forget where I was. And all of a sudden I'd be in Forest Park [St. Louis], lying on the grass like I used to . . . thinking. Then a machine gun would open you, and you couldn't make up your mind where you were—in St. Louis, or out in this beat-up jungle. And when the order came to get up and charge, you'd just go ahead—half of you in Forest Park and half on Hill 660. *

The Corps in these rugged conditions on New Britain, fighting not only a fanatical enemy but also the formidable jungle and weather conditions, produced, and continue to develop, outstand-

---

* George McMillian, *The Old Breed*, 202-203.

ing combat leaders of men. The adversities truly showed the kind of men we had.

Lt. Col. Lewis "Silent Lew" Walt took over the Third Battalion Fifth Marines in the midst of a heavy swamp after the Third lost its commander. Their objective was a heavily defended, strategic ridge in a wooded area that the Japanese code named Aogori. Lieutenant Colonel Walt personally led the action of his battalion, helping manhandle a half-ton 37mm cannon into place that swept the Japanese lines only ten yards away with deadly canister fire. For his outstanding leadership example, the next day when General Shepherd visited the battlefield, he declared, "From now on this ridge will be called Walt's Ridge."

Captain Joe Buckley commanded Weapons Company Seventh Marines. He also personally led his unit with reckless daring and abandonment in his own half-track. It included two light tanks, a jeep, and several 37mm guns. This unorthodox force performed exploits under heavy fire and driving rain clearing the base of Hill 660 of the enemy for the final successful assault that captured the hill. Buckley, who joined the Corps as a private in 1915, was decorated with the Navy Cross.

The legendary Chesty Puller, holder of five Navy Crosses in his lifetime, then a lieutenant colonel, led fast moving patrols into the interior mountains of Western New Britain in hot pursuit of the enemy.

Mitch Paige, who earned the Medal of Honor and a battlefield commission on Guadalcanal, also led his unit through the battle. In subsequent wars after World War II, MOH recipients would never be allowed to continue risking their lives in further combat because of their value to the nation as a living treasure.

At the end of our four arduous months in the Green Inferno we were relieved by the US Army's Fortieth Infantry Division. They unloaded their fine equipment and supplies as the raggedy A First loaded up on the same ships to be taken to another tropical paradise, Pavuvu—see next chapter. I can't help but wonder two things. First, what those fortunate Doggies did and how long they stayed in that tropical resort? Second, did they ever miss any of their vehicles marked with a pair of dice after they met the greatest scroungers in the world? That is another story for another time.

One week before the first echelons of the First Division boarded ship to depart, an unexpected visitor arrived aboard the cruiser *Nashville*. McMillan gives these insights in his inimitable report:

[T]he cruiser *Nashville* . . . was the largest naval vessel anyone had seen thereabouts since December. And about dusk word came from the beach master that General MacArthur was ashore. He soon arrived at Division CP. "The General shook hands all around," recalls a man who was there. "He was very affable and gave you the impression that he was very glad to see you again (although he had never seen you before)." The handshaking and the picture (the General brought photographers with him) did not take two minutes. The party then departed for the beach to re-embark. This was General MacArthur's first and last visit to Cape Gloucester during the time the First Marine Division was there. *

So much for the Great One! The last man in the First Marine Division departed the Green Inferno on 4 May 1944. Strangely, in researching and recording this story, it is as if I have been allowed by God to revisit that remote island. I feel my words are so inadequate to express both my inner feelings and the events that took place. But it is all I have.

Those of us who were there salute our fallen comrades. As we can never forget you, so we can never forget New Britain. Both are stamped indelibly in our hearts, minds, emotions, and bodies.

---

* George McMillian, *The Old Breed*, 227.

FOURTEEN

PAVUVU, ISLAND
OF DESTINY

Endure Discipline

Set an example of discipline and perfect steadiness under fire.
—*Lord Kitchener*

The men of the First Marine Division would like to have it explained why they remember more vividly the times they lived on a small island named Pavuvu than they do some of their most intense moments of combat.

—*The Old Breed History*

P avuvu: tiny dot in the Pacific. Largest of the Russell Islands, a part of the Solomon group. There were no battles fought there. A Marine Raider Battalion took these islands in 1943 with no opposition. Still, Pavuvu was an island of destiny for thousands of men from the First Marine Division.

The Division called Pavuvu home twice—after the battle of Cape Gloucester, New Britain, it was a staging area for combat on Peleliu. Then after Peleliu, before the battle of Okinawa. Pavuvu was an island of destiny for the First, partly because it was the last home on earth for 2,236 First Division Marines killed on both Peleliu and Okinawa. In these two battles an additional 11,887 were wounded in action and 114 were missing in action. On Okinawa, the Sixth Marine Division and four US Army divisions also suffered extremely heavy casualties.

Pavuvu has an abundance of rugged but good memories in my life: the camaraderie of unforgettable men; building company streets and battalion roads out of quarried coral, often hauled by steel helmet brigades; water shortages; C Company VSS. B Company basketball games, where I got into my first fist fight as a new Christian; the outdoor battalion movie amphitheater, where the seating was on coconut logs (or bring your own box); and the First's legendary, but losing battle against the island's droves of land crabs and rats.

During my twenty-six months overseas with the First Marine Division, I received two "Dear John" letters. They were heartbreakers. Within the first few months of being gone, a Dear John came from Pat, a diminutive, pretty blonde from my hometown. Though we were teenagers, we had a very serious relationship that began when she was fourteen and I was fifteen. Before I left for war we were engaged.

But there was an auxiliary relationship with Mary, a beautiful, fiery brunette from Los Angeles that seemed to develop well by correspondence after the breakup with Pat.

It turned out to be an infatuation, a wartime short-term sort of thing. Several months before we arrived on Pavuvu, Mary also broke my heart with an apologetic, lengthy Dear John. I was swimming in blood, for she was marrying a Marine lieutenant. I was only a PFC. Tragically, he was killed in action only a short time later.

One of my most vivid memories of Pavuvu was, about four months after Mary's Dear John, receiving a fruitcake from her with a loving note enclosed. The mail had taken so long to catch up with us that though she had sent the fruitcake long before her Dear John, it had disintegrated into a pile of crumbs—and she was already married! I shared her note, the crumbs and my bleeding heart with my tent mates in our eight-man tent and we ate in celebration of Mary's marriage! So went my life in wartime on scenic Pavuvu.

Perhaps there never has been an area where Marines were quartered that has been the subject of so much grumbling as Pavuvu. The island was chosen for the division after the battle of Cape Gloucester by staff officers of the Third Amphibious Corps as they flew over it! They viewed the beautiful shoreline and the six hundred acres of symmetrical rows of coconut palms that must have given them a feeling of tidiness about the place that a closer view would have betrayed.

It was up to the debilitated, combat-worn men of the First Marine Division Reinforced, minus casualties, to build a livable camp in this damp, soggy floor-mat of decaying coconuts which could not be harvested because of the war. We lived in eight-man tents strung between the tall, stately palms and soon became highly aware of the danger of falling coconuts. Several severe cases of concussion brought the awarding of the "Pavuvu Purple Heart"— medical treatment and a T.S. (tough situation) chit.

The First Tank Battalion, as well as the three infantry regiments and 11th Artillery Regiment, trained between the rows of palm trees on an adjacent island. As every man in our tank battalion knew, certain 40-foot-tall palm trees were pushovers when hit with a thirty-ton tank. Others were stubborn, with absolutely no give. Herman Sarubin found this out. He lost the most beautiful set of front teeth in C Company against the steel driver's hatch. These trees with no-give also fought back, by showering down coconuts on the hapless tank crews.

It was lonely.

To help ease the loneliness and to build up morale, the division showed movies and sometimes training films before the feature reel. I'll never forget one training film called *The Lost Company B*, developed by the Army. The essence of the film was that Company B was decimated in jungle combat because of a lack of discipline. One soldier had failed to get new shoelaces. His negligence caused blisters and infection when the old laces broke. He was the company runner and consequently could not get the message through which might have saved B Company from annihilation. The ancient proverb tells us, *"For want of a nail, a kingdom was lost."*

I have often thought of the spiritual application to the undisciplined *Lost Company B* film. In matters of the spirit there is a price to pay for neglecting the seemingly small or insignificant necessities. God often speaks to us through "a still, small voice" (1 Kings 19:12) or through the sound of a light whisper.

He tells us through our conscience that we ought to pray or to read the Bible and believe—or to obey this or not to do that. To neglect that "sound of gentle stillness" is sin, according to St. James, *"Anyone, then, who knows the good he ought to do and doesn't do it, sins"* (James 4:17).

FIFTEEN

A ROCK TOUGHER THAN BLOODY NOSE RIDGE

Peleliu, Island of Judgment

No man can answer for his courage who has never been in danger.

—Rochefoucald

I've been on Peleliu three times. The first time was during combat in 1944. After the battle I thought I'd never return. After all, it was an unknown island in the middle of the vast Pacific. But I did return. Twice. History and memories beckoned.

My second visit to Peleliu was forty-one years later, in November 1985. It was hard to believe that I was in a small motor launch, again headed for a landing on that memorable island. This trip was quiet and serene. The first was constant noise, smoke, and devastation.

I returned with LeRoy Eims, the Marine whose story is told in Chapter Seventeen, "He Died Looking Me Straight in the Eyes." LeRoy and I didn't know each other at the time of the invasion, though we were both in the First Marine Division and both were wounded on Peleliu. We met several years after the battle while we both worked for the same international Christian organization, The Navigators.

This was also LeRoy's second visit; there were ten of us in all. One was a Japanese friend of mine, Toru Nagai, whom I had met and discipled during my thirty-three years as a missionary in Japan, the land of my former enemies.

117

Riding in that motor launch four decades later, I thought deeply of the over 16,000 casualties of both sides on this tiny island. It seemed as though the living God had bought together some of the finest and bravest men from both nations, exposing them to a taste of living and dying hell. In an act of supreme judgment God allowed them to wound, maim, and kill one another. His judgment was twofold: upon individual young men, and also upon both nations as they were deprived of their sons. As men fell by bullet, bomb, and shell, Isaiah 3:35 came alive again: *"Thy men shall fall by the sword, and thy mighty in the war."*

Landing on Peleliu again, the memories kept flooding in. One of my chief feelings was a heart of thanksgiving to God for allowing me to be a survivor. Peleliu is basically a coral island and, therefore, during combat there is little chance to dig in—so there is very little protection from mortar and artillery shells, which also do not dig in before exploding and sending out their "daisy-cutter" shrapnel and coral fragments.

During my return, I stood on that airstrip that we had so furiously fought for and won, and remembered one day in 1944 when I was at the edge of the coral strip after we had captured it. I heard the *swoosh*—"insistent, intimate, as if it bore a secret that could not wait to be told"—of an incoming Japanese artillery shell. I hit the airstrip simultaneously with the projectile. Two men were killed nearby as the shell landed a few yards away. Hot shrapnel and spinning coral flew in every direction. I sustained a flesh wound in the arm, but not serious enough to be evacuated. As I came stumbling out of the rubble and smoke, covered with coral dust, my buddies thought I was a ghost. They thought for sure I had been killed. A Navy corpsman bound me up, and back into combat I went, though greatly shaken.

Psychologist Paul Tournier said, *"The adventurous life is not one exempt from fear, but on the contrary, one that is lived in full knowledge of fears of all kinds—one in which we go forward in spite of our fears."* How could we go forward in spite of our fears? That was a tough admonition to obey on Peleliu in the shadow of Bloody Nose Ridge. I was a new Christian, about one year old in the faith, during the battle of Peleliu. My way to move forward, in spite of fear, was to use the protection of a Rock even tougher and stronger than Bloody Nose Ridge. My security and safety during those fierce battles was in Psalm Eighteen. There I discovered a Rock higher than both the enemy and me. As often as I could during the battle, in my makeshift foxhole or in my tank, I read and meditated on Psalm Eighteen.

And, again, every day on our 1985 visit, for one week in the Palau Islands, I read and reread Psalm Eighteen. It contains a description of what has to be Peleliu-type combat. In the midst of intense battle, four times the entire Psalm speaks of the living God as the Rock of the true believer. Psalm 18:2–3 says, *"The Lord is my rock, and my fortress, and my deliverer, my God, my rock, in whom I take refuge, my shield and the horn of my salvation, my stronghold. I call upon the Lord, who is worthy to be praised, and I am saved from my enemies."*

In the midst of real fear—whether it be Peleliu-sized or much smaller—we can always count on taking refuge in the Rock. He is tougher than any of our problems and fears. He is, in the person of Jesus Christ, a shield and a stronghold. He asks us the question, *"Why are you afraid, O men of little faith?"* Christ is also a Stone of stumbling and a Rock of offense to the disobedient. He can be either a Rock that protects or a Rock that crushes.

To be on Peleliu again with Toru Nagai, a Japanese, was a highlight. Nagai was born one year before the battle. Somewhere in the South Pacific, perhaps on Peleliu, he lost an uncle; his father's brother never returned to Japan and his remains have never been found.

Nagai said during this trip,

I'm glad that these two soldiers, Boardman and Eims, lived and are sharing the gospel. Praise God that they survived. My father's youngest brother died somewhere in the Pacific. He was not a Marine-type. He never made a good soldier. He was a peaceful man, wrote poetry and songs—yet, he died in this part of the world. This brings me a very sad feeling. I can say deep in my heart I'm glad Japan's fascism ended. I think we must keep this peace forever. I'm going to tell the Japanese people these things. The best way I can contribute is to make the gospel true while I'm living. Helping disciple young people in Christ is the only hope I can have.

The third time I returned was on the fiftieth anniversary of Peleliu's D-Day, 15 September 1994. There were about two hundred Marine veterans and wives. The native Palauans hailed the returning Marine veterans with public signs that said, "Welcome Liberators, A Grateful Nation Remembers," and with public feasts, celebrations, and native dances. An emotional highlight was the Memorial Service at the First Marine Division monument on Bloody Nose Ridge. A Medal of Honor recipient, Capt. Everett Pope, who commanded Company C, First Battalion, First Regiment, stood at the makeshift podium and pointed at the steep coral ridge to the rear of us, saying, "I led ninety men up that ridge and came back with nine."

Part of Everett Pope's MOH citation read,

> He rallied his men and gallantly led them to the summit [of Hill 100] in the face of machine gun, mortar, and sniper fire . . . and for holding there although attacked continuously with grenades, machine guns, and rifles from three sides and twice subjected to suicidal charges during the night. He and his valiant men fiercely beat back or destroyed the enemy, resorting to hand-to-hand combat as the supply of ammunition dwindled and still maintaining his lines with his eight remaining riflemen when daylight brought more deadly fire and he was ordered to withdraw.

Some military strategists decry the value of the Peleliu battle. They say the island could have been bypassed, but hindsight is always 20/20. Who really knows. Fifty years after the battle, some Palauans gave a letter to one of the returning Marines veterans (he was Fred Coblentz, who was wounded on the fourth day of battle). Part of the letter reads,

Rage, Rage, Rage, engulfed the Pacific Islands fifty years ago and this week commemorated the carnage in Palau as American Veterans returned to its battlegrounds. I wonder if we were able to truly honor them for what they did then and what was to follow over the next half century. Had Palau been bypassed by the American forces would there be a Palau today; would there be a people called Palauans?

Lest we forget, Palau was forcibly taken by Japan eighty years ago this month. Some two years lapsed before the League of Nations mandated the Micronesian Islands to Japan with the proviso of non-militarization. America refused membership in that body and refused recognition of the mandate.

After the bloody battles of the Palau, the US military initiated a benevolent restoration of the islands followed by an agreement with the United Nations to oversee the development of self-determination for the peoples of Micronesia.

In a few days we Palauans will join the world of nations with all of the privileges and the responsibilities which come with our new political status. As the American veterans depart the islands, we Palauans should reflect upon the events of the days commemorating our liberation as well as examine what might have been had these veterans not come in 1944.

I say to those veterans of the Battles of Palau, thank you, thank you, thank you; were it not for you, freedom for our people would not have come. God Speed.

—*Roman Tmetuchl, 16 September 1994*

Farewell, Peleliu! We will probably never see you again, but we can never forget you. Farewell, our comrades who gave their all! You are unforgettable patriots and men among men. You are the epitome of Semper Fidelis.

SIXTEEN

"FRIENDLY" TANKS HELP A MARINE PRAY

A Close Call with Death on Peleliu

He prayed as if God were at his elbow.

—*Anonymous*

PFC Claude Franklin landed on Peleliu on D-Day, September 15, 1944. He was a gunner in the 60mm Mortar Section of I Company, Third Battalion, Fifth Regiment of the First Marine Division. He gives this account of how prayer saved his life:

I'll never forget the D-Day landing on Peleliu.

As we neared the beachhead, the amphibious tractor that carried my squad got stuck on a huge mass of underwater coral. Shells were bursting everywhere. I saw several other amphibs burning in the water and on the beach. I was scared.

We jumped over the side into the surf, hunkered down and then literally crawled ashore. Immediately, I heard a command, "Get those mortars set up and firing!"

I looked at my mortar tube and it had sand in it. I reached back to get the cleaning staff off my pack and it wasn't there. The mortar wouldn't fire unless I could get the sand out of the tube. I looked behind me, thinking *I might have dropped the staff while crawling up the beach.* Almost in panic. I prayed, "Lord, help me find that cleaning staff!" I spotted it in the surf! I scrambled back and got it. We hastily swabbed out the tube and moments later had it firing.

Shortly we moved inland amidst terrible noise, smoke, and confusion. We realized that we had been separated from the rest of our company. This increased my fear and panic. Then we heard a lot of noise and machine gun fire *behind* us. We spotted two US Sherman tanks and felt somewhat relieved . . . for a few seconds.

Then we realized that these tanks were headed right toward us, shooting up everything in front of them with their machine guns and 75mm cannon. Either we had strayed out into "No Man's Land" or the tanks had come in behind us instead of on our flank. Someone yelled, "Let's get out of here!" All of the mortar section, except myself and Ed Mahoney, took off running laterally away from the tanks.

Mahoney and I found a partial cover behind a small pile of coral rocks. We felt if we stood up to run, the gunner in the tank would mow us down before he realized we were Marines. He was traversing back and forth with machine gun fire and occasional blasts from his cannon.

I was terrified, thinking, *This is it. I'm going to die.* Then a thought flashed in my mind, something I had learned years before from Psalm 124:8, *"Our help is in the name of the Lord, who made heaven and earth."* So I started praying, "Lord, be with us. Please help us, Lord,"

Mahoney and I were flat on our bellies behind the rocks, which weren't more than eighteen inches high when the machine gun started spraying the rocks, sending coral chips and debris all over us. At the same time, a blast from the cannon literally lifted us off the ground. It dazed us for a few seconds, then Mahoney said, "I'm hit! I'm hit!" He put a hand to his eyes and brought it down covered with blood. Then I remembered the twenty-third Psalm, memorized in church school and started mentally reciting verse four: *"Yea though I walk through the valley of the shadow of death, I will fear no evil; for Thou art with me."*

This gave me a feeling of calmness and confidence that I hadn't had before. I seemed to feel the presence of God. Suddenly, the tank veered off at an angle. We crawled around the rocks, like squirrels around a tree, to keep from being seen. After the tank passed us, we ran up behind it and knocked on it, and it stopped.

This was my closest brush with death. Mahoney only had a small cut in one eyebrow, probably from a piece of flying rock. I suffered no injuries.

Did the Lord hear my prayer and turn that tank away from us or did it just happen that way? It can't be proven, but I believe it was because of my prayer. And I've been a strong believer in the power of prayer ever since.

In times of danger and death, as well as in seasons of peace, we need the resource of instant prayer. As with Claude Franklin, it ought to be as natural as breathing. Jesus prayed. He invites us to pray constantly. Someone once said, *"Prayer is not overcoming God's reluctance; it is laying hold of His highest willingness."*

Said S. Olford, *"There is only one thing that will save us in this hour of desperation, and that is prayer."*

SEVENTEEN

HE DIED LOOKING ME STRAIGHT IN THE EYES

The Marine Who Didn't Know How to Pray

The most momentous concern of man is the state he shall enter upon after this transitory life is ended.

—*Clarke*

My editor and close friend, Monte "Chuck" Unger wrote the following account of action in one sector of the landing beach at Peleliu. May the challenge of this story grip your heart as it did mine.

On September 15, 1944, the First Marine Division assaulted the coral island of Peleliu in the western Carolines.

Nineteen-year-old PFC Ivan LeRoy Eims, a Marine radioman, manning a .30 caliber machine gun in B Company Third Armored Amphibious Tractor Battalion is in zero wave. That is *before* the first wave. The only people in front of him are the enemy, waiting. Japanese sitting behind their machine guns, by their mortars. Watching. The silent, hidden enemy.

The amphibs thunder across the coral reef and the Japanese begin firing. And hitting. Stakes in the coral and stakes out in the water, all placed earlier by Colonel Nakagawa's soldiers, mark off the exact distance for the Japanese mortar men. Before D-Day is over, these Marines will lose one-half of their vehicles. Many of them were sitting ducks. In the first eight days of fighting, some units will lose sixty percent of their men, wounded and dead.

Eim's tank touches sand and dashes onto the beach. A Japanese shell rips completely through the tank. Sliding steel doors hidden in a coral cave somewhere on Bloody Nose Ridge had quietly opened. A Japanese artilleryman has the amphib squarely in his sights. A direct hit.

Eims yells, "Let's get out of here!"

They get. And fast.

The Marines on the beach are being ripped apart.

Eims passes one man whose stomach is completely blown away. Only a thin piece of skin on each of his sides holds him together. Peleliu will be no pushover.

Eims is racing for cover, ready to do battle, now as an infantryman. The sand in front of him pops, pops, pops. A machine gun sprays a burst of bullets at him.

"As soon as that strip was laid down, I ran for cover. I didn't get far when I saw what the machine gunner had just hit."

A Marine lays in a pool of blood. He had been riddled from his ankles to his throat by the burst. Lying there. About to die.

The wounded Marine grabs Eims. "Mate, I need help."

Then the wounded man says, "Do you know how to pray?"

"Pray? I didn't know how to pray. I didn't know anything about religion. Nothing. But there was a fellow crawling along a little ridge just above us. I reached up and grabbed him, pulled him down and asked, 'Do you know how to pray?' He cussed me out. I had the wrong guy. When I turned back to the wounded man, he died looking me straight in the eyes."

Eims could offer no help.

"I didn't know how to help him. That machine gun could have gotten me. A few more feet. I began wondering what happens to a guy when he dies. I wondered where that dead Marine went when he died. I didn't know, but I was sure of one thing, I was going to find out."

But the war goes on. Eims stumbles over another wounded Marine. This one has his upper lip shot off. No upper lip, yet he is trying to smoke a cigarette.

While Eims and a corpsman help the man, a Jeep comes up behind them and is hit.

"That Jeep literally disappeared, and the two riders with it. There wasn't one large piece of anything left. Just smoke. But some of the shrapnel of that explosion hit me. There was a hole in my left knee about the size of a lemon. An artery was hanging out, like a little finger, hanging out of my knee and pumping blood on the ground in rhythm, like a heartbeat."

Eims shouts, "I'm hit."

The corpsman he is with is hit too. His left arm blown off. Staggering over to Eims, he says in an apologetic tone, "I'm sorry, but I don't think I'll be able to help you." Then he keels over. Dead.

Eims is finally evacuated to a hospital ship.

The Marines go on to eventually take Peleliu. It turned out to be one of the bloodiest battles in the Pacific.

After the war, Eims got a job as a telegrapher in a railway depot in Harlan, Iowa. He never forgot those haunting eyes of that dying young infantryman on Peleliu. The war had quenched Eims's thirst for adventure, but there was another, more gnawing thirst. What is life really all about?

Eims eventually learned the meaning of life through reading the Bible. He became a Christian and devoted the rest of his life to reaching and influencing others for Christ.

The question asked by the dying Marine, "Do you know how to pray?" is one we must all face. For him it was too late. For us, the living, even in the twilight of life, it is never too late. The disciples said to Jesus, "Lord, teach us to pray." He answered their request. He will also answer yours.

EIGHTEEN

IF HELL HAD AN ANNEX
IT WAS PELELIU

Transferring Unnecessary Guilt

Guilt upon the conscience, like rust upon iron, both defiles and consumes it, gnawing and creeping into it, as that does which at last eats out the very heart and substance of the metal.

—*South*

Peleliu, a two-by-six-mile island, part of the Palau Group in the Western Carolines, just seven degrees off the equator, had one of the bloodiest battles in the Pacific for the First Marine Division—6,336 casualties, including 1,121 killed. I received my first Purple Heart there, but this story is about George Head, a comrade in the First.

George had been a veteran of Guadalcanal and Cape Gloucester, New Britain, before his landing on Peleliu on 15 September 1944. He was an infantryman squad leader in Company A, First Battalion, First Marine Regiment commanded by the legendary Col. Chesty Puller.

In the first three days of the battle of Peleliu, the regiment lost 1,236 men, nearly half its strength. When the unit came off the lines on 23 September, the First Battalion had sustained seventy-percent casualties. "We're not a regiment," said one of the men that day. "We're the survivors of a regiment."

Before embarking for the invasion from the island of Pavuvu, divisional engineers had set up a carpenter shop. "Outside was an ever-lengthening line of chaste wooden crosses stacked against each other ready to be loaded for Peleliu."

George came very close to earning one of those white crosses. Here, in his own words, is the amazing story of this honest, God-fearing veteran. He tells of his survival, long-time struggle and victory over guilt.

Our platoon hit the beach of Peleliu about 10:30 a.m. on September 15, 1944. There was a tremendous amount of confusion because of the heavy Japanese mortar, machine gun, and small arms fire. We were scattered and disorganized. Platoon Sgt. Bob Sewell finally got us together. My squad had lost contact with the rest of the second platoon and the other squads of Company A. As we moved up from the beach, the jungle scrub was thick and heavy.

I don't recall how my squad got back together but we did move out from the scrub into more open ground. As I looked behind me, I could count only five or six of my thirteen-man squad. There were more, but I could not see them because of the rough terrain.

We halted at a point about five hundred to six hundred yards from our objective, "Bloody Nose Ridge." The Ridge was an ugly mass of shell-torn coral with a broken, shattered landscape. It looked like something from Dante's *Inferno*.

At that point, I froze and looked back. The other men seemed to freeze, too, waiting for someone to move them out.

I couldn't move, but felt a strange fear I hadn't experienced on Guadalcanal or Cape Gloucester . . . I was scared! Had I turned "yellow"? I didn't go backward, but I couldn't move forward. I just crouched there, hoping our planes, ships, or heavy artillery would kill the Japanese so I wouldn't have to do it.

Minutes later, to my right, Captain Jennings, our Company Commander, came up beside me. He looked at me and ordered, "Keep moving out."

As he said that, I got up to move and was hit in the neck. I had a sensation of dizziness, the ground swelling up to meet me, of falling in a whirling dream. To my left was a shell hole. Knowing I was hit, I dove into the hole to keep from being wounded again. And, then, in a state of semiconsciousness, I offered up a prayer, *"Dear God, if it's time for me to die . . . help me die like a man."*

Why I said this particular prayer I didn't know then. It might have been a feeling of guilt for not moving my squad, or the look in Captain Jennings's eyes when he spoke to me. Whatever the reasons, I had a feeling of guilt and I carried that feeling for a number of years after the war.

Not until much later, while talking with the men of Company A at reunions, did I realize that others had experienced the same or similar feelings in combat. I had not "bugged out," yet I had a dark image and vague fear that I had. I was just one of many who were scared, and many others reacted as I did.

But time heals many wounds, physical and emotional. I owe a debt of gratitude to all the fine men of Company A and many others who helped me work through this problem.

I am proud to have served with such brave Marines.

I know now that my *main enemy* was not the Japanese on that day of hell on Peleliu. My real enemy was subconscious guilt.

Christ said, *"Come unto me all you who are burdened and heavy laden and I will give you rest."* He has given me peace with myself and a permanent freedom from guilt, which was my real enemy.

NINETEEN

REQUIEM FOR A HEAVYWEIGHT

Commitment beyond the Call of Duty

I do not think a braver gentleman . . . more daring or bold, is now alive.

—*William Shakespeare Henry IV, Part 1*

P vt. Charles "Chick" Owen knew that this was the day he would die.

He was a sixteen-year-old Marine pinned down by Japanese gunfire on Peleliu's "Orange Beach Three." It was early morning, D Day, 15 September 1944.

Owen was in one of the first waves of Marines to land. He was flat on his stomach in the white sand. Ahead of him the dark jungle and coral ridges were filled with over ten thousand Japanese trying to kill him. Behind him more and more Marines were coming in. He couldn't go back and was too scared to go forward.

Though all combat Marines had been trained over and over to get off an exposed beach, Owen and his teenage buddies were frozen in fear. Owen said, *"Everyone on that beach prayed, either desperately to themselves or out loud."* They felt it would be suicide to move.

Owen saw torn bodies and body parts strewn around him while bullets were zinging over his head and hitting in the sand beside him. He was seeing and hearing the realities of war, not the romantic, exciting picture he had imagined when he lied about his age and had joined the Marines in Georgia two years earlier at age fourteen! Owen was positive that he and his buddies would not survive the first day of battle.

Everyone on the beach was stretched out flat so they wouldn't be a target for the Japanese. No one would stand up. That would be certain death. Those who did move forward into the jungle crawled as low to the ground as they could.

Owen said, "The noise of the incoming fire was such that voice contact was almost impossible; the artillery, antitank, mortar, machine gun, and other small arms fire was dealing out death by the wholesale upon the assaulting Marines and particularly to those who remained on the beach."

Then Owen saw something he couldn't believe. There was a man standing up, walking right toward him and his praying buddies. He was a Marine major from some other company. Owen didn't know him. The officer was armed with a Tommy gun and had a Japanese shovel slung over his shoulder. This mysterious officer, outwardly fearless, had his Major's insignia in plain sight on his collar, rather than hidden on the underside where it would not attract enemy snipers.

As the major came toward the young Marines, Owen said, "I heard a voice, a very loud voice. I would describe it as a booming voice, one that could be heard over all the accompanying noises of battle, one I would never forget. It still rings in my ears today: 'Get off this beach or I'll shoot your butt!'" It was the major yelling at us. His commanding presence, courage under fire, and bravery were the answer to the young Marines' prayers. It was either the wrath of the unknown major or the Japanese mortars. The choice was easy. The men moved inland on the double.

Owen later learned that the next mortar barrage exploded precisely where they had been lying. He says, "If that major hadn't been on that beach, on his own, no one having told him to do it, I would have been dead right there, at age sixteen."

Charles Owen and his outfit moved inland taking bloody yard after yard from the enemy who had pledged to fight to the death. That same night those persistent Japanese mortar shells, which had been unable to hit Owen on the beach, finally caught up with him. Wounded in the neck he was evacuated to a hospital ship for a short time, but soon rejoined what remained of A Company, First Battalion, Seventh Regiment of the First Marine Division and finished out the battle of Peleliu.

Owen served the Marine Corps for over twenty-two years, went through three wars and retired as a master sergeant. During all of those years and long after his retirement he often wondered who the mysterious major was who had saved their lives on Peleliu. Throughout all of Charles Owen's battles and experiences in the Corps, which included Okinawa after Peleliu, North China, Korea, and Vietnam, he says, *I have seen many, many deeds of heroism in combat, but none even closely compare with the performance of that major on the beach at Peleliu.*

Finally, all of the pieces of the puzzle of the "mysterious major" were put together for Owen. W. H. "Brock" Brockinton, a Marine rifle platoon and company commander in the battle of Okinawa, had read Charles Owen's account of this incident in Bill Ross's book, *Peleliu: Tragic Triumph.* Brockinton immediately knew that the unknown major was his close friend from Charleston, South Carolina, Arthur M. Parker Jr., Lt. Col. USMC Retired.

During the Marine Corps first amphibious landing in World War II, the battle of Guadalcanal, Arthur Parker had been the company commander of B Company, First Battalion, Seventh Regiment, under Lt. Col. Chesty Puller, until Parker was wounded and evacuated. For the Peleliu landing Parker had been assigned as executive officer of the Third Armored Amphibious Battalion. He was a tough, experienced, nondiplomatic, but good-hearted, officer who had shaped his troops into an effective fighting force prior to the attack on Peleliu.

Brockinton arranged for Owen and Parker to meet. In October 1992, forty-eight years after D-Day on Peleliu, Charles Owen finally met the mysterious major face to face. Owen said of Parker, "The major's physical appearance had naturally changed considerably, but that same booming voice was still a part of him, and I picked up on it immediately. It is hard for me to describe how emotional this meeting was. It was probably the most emotional event of my life." It had taken forty-eight years to identify Arthur "Ace" Parker as the hero on that beachhead.

Parker remembered, "I was trying to get things back together on this beach and that is when I ran into the infantry. There was a whole conglomeration of troops in one place—a dead target for the Japanese artillery and mortars. Although I had nothing to do with these infantrymen, other than to help them, they had to be gotten off that beach or they would all have been killed. After all these years to think that I would be remembered for this incident makes my whole life worthwhile."

Later in the Peleliu campaign, Parker was awarded the Bronze Star with Combat V for leading elements of the Third Armored Amphibious Battalion on the assault of nearby Ngesebus Island. There is no doubt that he should have also been appropriately decorated for the beachhead action, but fellow officer, Lt. Wilson T. Bristol, a Navy Cross recipient who would have been able to make the recommendation, was killed himself on Peleliu that very same morning.

Rob Wood, a former Marine and friend of mine has said, *"It is not important what is chiseled into a man's tombstone—it is what he left chiseled into the hearts of those that follow later that is important."* Parker was a heavyweight among Marines. Of all the outstanding warriors serving in the Corps, his name should be listed among the more distinguished. This simple, but sincere requiem tribute for Arthur M. Parker Jr., one of America's great soldier-patriots, is a reminder of God's great love and sacrifice for us.

The desperate, sincere prayers for deliverance, offered by young Charles Owen and his teenage buddies on Peleliu's fire-swept Orange Beach Three were unexpectedly answered by the appearance of Major Parker, a God-fearing man. Parker was willing to put himself in great jeopardy, even to sacrifice his own life, to help inexperienced young Marines live and fight on.

We were helpless under the onslaught of the vicious enemy of our souls when Jesus Christ actually laid down His life for us. He died in our place. He took our sins upon Himself, then rose from the dead to give us the hope of eternal life. He never disregards the sincere cry of our hearts for help, mercy, and forgiveness.

"This is how we know what love is: Jesus Christ laid down his life for us. And we ought to lay down our lives for our brothers" (1 JOHN 3:16).

I received this letter from Harvey Weinstein after he had read this chapter printed earlier in my chaplain's corner:

Reading "Requiem for a Heavyweight" brought back vivid and chilling memories of 9/15/44. I was the radio machine gunner in Maj. "Ace" Parker's Command tank and the memory of the landing and aftermath are etched in my mind. It might be of interest to know that from one of the antennas, we flew, at Parker's orders, the Confederate flag. We were hit approaching the beach, got hung up on a coral reef, pulled off by another of our tanks, hit again in the shallows, and finally disabled as we reached the beach, when Major Parker ordered us to abandon the tank.

I spent most of the morning with "Ace" and can certainly attest to his incredible bravery and total disregard for his personal safety, as well as his booming voice as we dug down into the sand waiting for the first wave to reach us. Like Charles Owen, I, too, was a very frightened young (nineteen) Marine. I know that Major Parker saved my life, as well as many others that fateful day.

I remained with Major Parker through Peleliu and also the Okinawa operation and have countless memories of our time together, and was deeply saddened by his recent death.

TWENTY

ANGELS IN HELL'S ANNEX

Navy Corpsmen Among The Marines

The angels may have wider spheres of action and nobler forms
of duty than ourselves, but truth and right to them and to us are
one and the same thing.

—E. H. Chapin

Were there angels on Peleliu, Hell's Annex? Death, the King
of Terrors, held court on that two-by-six mile jungle-covered, coral outcropping in the Pacific. He held out his scepter beckoning forth over ten thousand Japanese young men. No one has
ever known the exact count except the King of Terrors and Almighty God Himself.

King Death was more selective with the 28,484 men of the
First Marine Division Reinforced. Before the invasion, the division
had estimated five hundred Marine casualties on D-Day. Who can
outguess Death and his careful plan? The first day on that narrow
and precariously held beachhead, it cost us over twice as many
casualties, 1,298: 1,148 wounded, ninety-two killed and fifty-eight
missing in action.

The commanding general of the First Marine Division had issued a communiqué four days before embarking for Peleliu from
Guadalcanal. It stated with great confidence and certainty that
Peleliu would be a *"short one, a quickie. Rough but fast. We'll be
through in three days. It might take only two."* Instead of short, fast
and hard, it was slow, hard, and long!

Capt. George Hunt of Company K, First Marine Regiment, came
ashore with 235 men. Three days later after the ferocious and pre-

carious battle for the Point, Company K went into reserve with a remnant of seventy-eight men. Our C Company, First Tank Battalion Company Commander, Capt. John Heath, was riding on the back of one of our tanks, directing fire. The King's scepter was held out to him, his name was called. A sniper shot him between the eyes.

John Heath was one of our finest officers, a tough, disciplined, no-nonsense captain who had come up through the ranks, a "mustang." On the island of Pavuvu, in preparation for the invasion of Peleliu, he had molded C Company into a well-trained, disciplined, tough outfit with high *esprit*. Upon news of his death, most of us couldn't believe that his name would be called! We should have known before Peleliu that the Grim Reaper is no respecter of persons.

If ever the men of the First Marine Division needed the help and intervention of angels, it was on this terrible island of judgment and multiplying casualties. The scorching heat was our enemy, too. Peleliu was only seven degrees off the equator. Each day we fought in 110-degree-plus heat. Every Marine came ashore with two full canteens of water, but once ashore these were quickly emptied. Water was extremely scarce, especially when the beachhead was so precarious. Some Marines low on water and ammunition had to resort to drawing brackish water from the bottom of shell holes with dead, decaying, bloated bodies only a few feet away.

A two or three-day struggle to capture the island? It took over one month for this grim struggle! In the end 1,252 Marines and 404 soldiers from the First Wildcat Division were selected to take the journey of no return.

Two kinds of angels landed on Peleliu with us. The first wore Marine uniforms, but were not Marines. Have you ever seen a Marine angel? Not impossible, but most improbable! It may be difficult for a Marine to admit, but the first kind of angel were Navy personnel. The US Navy, the finest floating force in the world, gave the Marines their best.

Doctors, corpsmen, and chaplains were well-trained angels of mercy. They offered us not only the finest of service physically and spiritually, but they also gave themselves sacrificially, often expending their very lives. Ask any combat Marine how he feels about these "docs," surgeons, chaplains, and Navy nurses aboard hospital ships. Many of us will say, without hesitation, that we would not be here today if it were not for these rough-clad, tough-talking angels of mercy.

WHO TAUGHT YOU, CORPSMAN?

Who taught you grimy corpsman?
You who first bound up the nation's wounded,
Kneeling on the battlefield,
A specialist in stanching blood
Who knows no bounds to valor.

Who taught you grimy corpsman,
The Hippocratic lies that the living tell the dying?
The gruff thumbs up,
The noncommittal nod.
Do you know you're lying?

Who taught you grimy corpsman,
To crawl out under deadly fire?
To ease the pain of the last few breaths
With cooling hands
And reassuring smile.

Who taught you grimy corpsman,
As you fight death in death's own grim arena?
I know who taught you grimy corpsman,
This compassion for the wounded
Must be taught by God.

—*Ken Gruebel*

Reprinted by permission of *Leatherneck Magazine.*

Tom Lea, a *Life* magazine war artist, landed on Peleliu fifteen minutes after the first wave on D Day, with Headquarters Company, Seventh Marine Regiment. He gives this vivid description of these Navy saviors in action that he came across in a huge shell hole on the narrow beachhead:

> About thirty paces back of the Japanese trench a sick bay had been established in a big shell crater made by one of our battle-ship guns. Laying around it were pieces of shrapnel over a foot long. In the center of the crater at the bottom a doctor was work-ing on the worst of the stretcher cases. Corpsmen, four to a stretcher, came in continually with their bloody loads. The doc-tor had attached plasma bottles to the top of a broken tree stump and was giving transfusions as fast as he could after rough sur-gery. Corpsmen plied tourniquets, sulfa, morphine, and handled the walking wounded and lighter cases with first aid.
>
> The padre stood by with two canteens and a Bible, helping. He was deeply and visibly moved by the patient suffering and death. He looked very lonely, very close to God, as he bent over the shattered men so far from home. Corpsmen put a poncho, a shirt, a rag, anything handy, over the gray faces of the dead and carried them to a line on the beach, under a tarpaulin, to await the digging of graves. *

There was a second kind of angel on Peleliu. In several cases the second type thought it good to team up with the first ones and give a helping, saving hand in the midst of the carnage of battle and death. They also had a penchant for dressing in Marine dun-garees and helmets. Here is the story of a corpsman with the Fifth Marine Regiment and his encounter with an angel of the second kind:

Joe Marquez from Los Angeles, a tall, athletic basketball Most Valuable-Player award winner and student-body president in high school, joined the Navy in 1943. In San Diego he underwent in-tense hospital corpsman training. Although he didn't know it at the time, all of that wartime medical preparation was for the one unforgettable battle of Peleliu.

---

* *Reporting World War II, Part Two: American Journalism 1944-1946* (The Li-brary of America, New York, 1995), 510, 512.

For extraordinary heroism on that rugged, coral island he would be awarded the Navy Cross, our nation's second highest award to Navy and Marine personnel.

The President of the United States takes pleasure in
presenting
The NAVY CROSS to
ELEUTERIO JOE MARQUEZ
PHARMACIST'S MATE THIRD CLASS
United States NAVAL RESERVE
For service as set forth in the following CITATION:

For extraordinary heroism as a Hospital Corpsman with an Assault Company attached to FIFTH Marines, FIRST Marine Division, in action against enemy Japanese forces on Peleliu, Palau Islands, on October 13, 1944. Although severely wounded in both legs during an action in which his company was subjected to intense hostile fire, MARQUEZ courageously dragged himself over extremely rough and difficult terrain to aid seven of his wounded comrades, and, although unable to walk, treated each of the casualties in turn, remaining with them and refusing treatment for himself until they were evacuated. His valiant devotion to duty and grave concern for the welfare of others were in keeping with the highest traditions of the United States Naval Service.
   —*For the President, James Forrestal, Secretary of the Navy*

Joe was an angel of mercy to Marines of the Fifth Marine Regiment. Several owe their lives to him. But in the midst of Peleliu's crisis, Joe encountered the second kind of angel. Here is the story in his own words not told in the official Citation:

I landed on Peleliu on 15 September 1944 with H and S Company. I was assigned to the battalion aid station. My job was to further treat and evacuate the wounded as they came off the lines. My first taste of fear and helplessness came as we were unloading supplies from the Amtrac. The mortar and artillery that we were receiving were terrible. Later that day we received another heavy shelling with many in H and S Company wounded and a few KIAs.

One of the Marines had an arm and leg blown off, and this affected me deeply because I could not save him. I thought about this Marine when I prayed, and although I felt that I would not be killed, I did have a feeling that I would be wounded. I prayed that I would not be disfigured or that I would not suffer the loss of a limb. The longer the campaign lasted the more I thought about the loss of a limb, and finally decided that if I had to lose a limb to please make it a leg. My father was a paraplegic and he was able to get around. I felt I could still work as long as I had my arms.

The first night on Peleliu I was unable to sleep but it did not matter as I was told to report to G-2-5. The next morning after we took the airfield, I found G Company and stayed with them for three weeks. I enjoyed working with the Marines. We seemed to form a bond. My only close call during that period was when we were hit by friendly fire and I received a small laceration on my forehead. After being relieved I returned to H and S Company, had some hot chow, and two good nights rest.

On 11 October 1944, I reported to Fox Company. I do not remember any names of the members of the platoon. The Lieutenant I remember only as "Meatball." That evening a mortar shell hit us and we had a couple of wounded, including the other corpsman. The following day we moved up onto Bloody Nose Ridge and hooked up with another platoon. We were still understaffed, but we did have three corpsmen and one lieutenant. About 4 a.m. on Friday the thirteenth, the Japanese were able to climb the ridge and lob some grenades into our lines. When a grenade exploded I felt my leg rise, and the first thing I thought about was the Marine that had lost his arm and leg. I was scared and I do not know what I would have done if the person next to me had not started yelling that he had been hit. I was able to calm this person and then I was able to do what I had been trained to do.

I began to crawl around to assess the damage to see who needed to be treated first. One of the corpsmen, named Ken, was the most seriously wounded and I decided to give him a unit of plasma. I could not see his veins in the dark and asked the lieutenant if we could get a flare sent over our area. His reply was, "You're in charge, Doc!" With the light from the flare, I was able to start the plasma. A Marine volunteered to watch the plasma so that I could take care of the other wounded. It was at this time that I heard a voice say, "I'm a corpsman, can I help?" I said yes and continued working.

At daylight some stretcher-bearers and a corpsman came on the scene and the corpsman said, "I hear you need help up here." I told him everyone was taken care of but that he could take care of me. I told him that another corpsman had come up to help me. He said, "That's impossible, we are the closest unit to you and we were just able to get up here." I don't know who that other corpsman was or where he came from. Maybe someday I will know who that angel from Heaven was that came to help me.

I told the stretcher-bearers to take Ken down first as he was the most serious. The other ones that could walk I told to just follow the stretcher. I looked at the lieutenant and again he said, "You're in charge, Doc!" I had the other leg wound taken care of next and then I had the lieutenant take the third stretcher. I did not know that there were only three stretchers so I had to be helped down the ridge by two Marines. The next morning, after surgery, Ken died. Even to this day I still relive this experience and give thanks to God for seeing me through this terrible campaign.

Joe concludes his story with these words: "My wife, Annette, others, and I claim that on that fateful night on Peleliu, with so much death, dying, and mutilation, that the other mysterious corpsman that helped me was a heavenly angel sent by God. I have to believe this until someone proves otherwise—and I don't think they will."

The Word of God that cannot lie speaks often of angels. *"The angel of the Lord guards and rescues all who reverence Him"* (Psalm 34:7).

These messengers of God are all around us living in what is to us the invisible world, but that which is truly the real world. *"Millions of spiritual creatures walk the earth unseen, both when we sleep and when we are awake,"* said John Milton. The limitations in our bodies of flesh prevent us from observing them except as God chooses to reveal their presence—as on Peleliu—to Joe Marquez and others for a short and crucial period of time.

Another Hospital Corpsman, Brooking Rouse Gex, of Welches, Oregon, reported the same miraculous phenomenon of the intervention of an angel *"of the second kind"* in the battle of Peleliu.

Christians should never fail to sense the operation of an angelic glory. It forever eclipses the world of demonic powers, as the sun does a candle light.

—*Billy Graham*

Peleliu. Marine reinforcements pass destroyed DUKW and Amtrac on sides. September 1944.

Peleliu. Japanese artillery piece in one of five hundred caves, both natural and man-made. Gun was named Harao.

Peleliu. Infantry and beach defenses, standing by to stand by.

Peleliu's coral airstrip. Three Sherman tanks amidst bombed out Japanese planes and hangers. I received my first Purple Heart in this area. Bloody Nose Ridge in background.

Peleliu airstrip. One of our C Company tanks with Japanese hanger skeleton in background. Steel tracks welded on front slope and turret for more protection.

Peleliu battlefield. Note infantrymen advancing—tank has been hit or thrown a track. Note two vehicles on causeway.

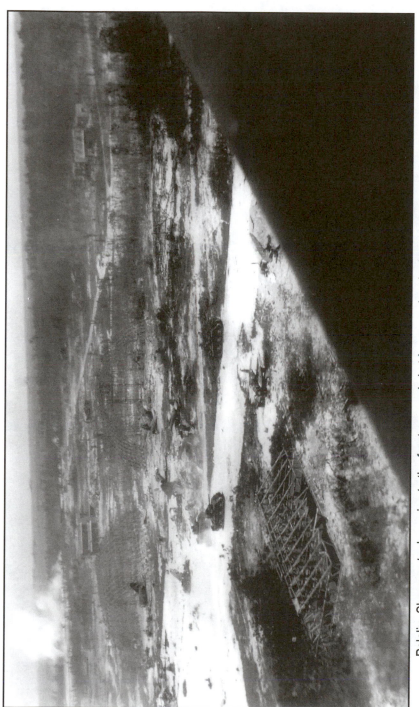

Peleliu. Sherman tank moving to the front on coral airstrip among bombed-out Japanese planes and hangers.

Peleliu. Armored vehicles, probably Amtracs, crossing from Ngesebus to Peleliu.

Peleliu. C Company bulldozer Sherman tank firing into caves.

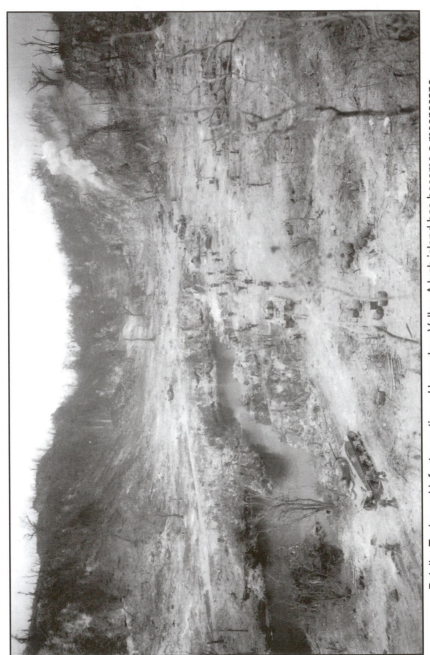

Peleliu. Tanks and infantry sortie up Horseshoe Valley. A lush island has become a moonscape.

Joe Marquez, Corpsman, Navy Cross, Peleliu. Chapter Eighteen.

V. OKINAWA: THE
LAST BATTLE

AUTHOR'S INTRODUCTION TO OKINAWA

Okinawa: The Last Battle

I was already living and working in missions on Okinawa in late 1952 and 1953 when Jean, my fiancée, came to Japan for our wedding. She came over on a twelve-passenger freighter. I went from Okinawa to Japan by Japanese ship to meet her. Ten days later we were married in Tokyo. We honeymooned in Atami, Japan, and Sun-Moon Lake, Taiwan.

When I took Jean to Okinawa in August 1953, it was only eight years after the battle. Conditions were still very primitive; the Okinawans were trying to recover from the most devastating war they had ever experienced. Well over one hundred thousand of the civilian population had perished—no one knows the exact number. The American government generously helped in the recovery.

For four years Jean and I lived in a small, rented Okinawan home with no running water. We caught rainwater in barrels for drinking and also used a well—but boiled all drinking and cooking water. For over a year we had electricity only at night and no refrigerator but a crude icebox. We slept under a mosquito net.

God had given us a heart for the Okinawan people and for their physical, emotional, and spiritual needs—and also for the US servicemen stationed on that narrow coral island. Our first two of five children, Holly and Laurel, were born in a Quonset hut.

Our four years living on Okinawa before moving to Japan were some of the greatest and most fruitful of our thirty-six years living overseas. Even today, by the grace of our great God, there are Okinawan people serving Him—some as pastors.

Living and working on the narrow confines of that former battlefield bought back such vivid memories. Off and on over that time I experienced recurring nightmares. Perhaps that would have happened in the homeland, too, but I'm sure being on Okinawa served to exacerbate it. In those days we had seldom heard of Post-Battle Traumatic Stress Syndrome (PTSD). We World War II Yanks may have gotten along a lot better by not knowing about those fancy nomenclatures!

Putting together this section on Okinawa has brought to the fore in my mind how little I knew about the overall battle when Jean and I lived there in the early '50s. As I researched Sugar Loaf Hill, I realized anew that our home, described above, was very near and probably on the backside of Crescent Hill! Truly it was all hallowed ground.

Every year on 17 June our family, alone or with a few friends, would take a lunch and hold a memorial and thanksgiving service at Kunishi Ridge on the spot where our tanks were knocked out. Not only fighting on Okinawa, but also living there later made those unforgettable times live more vividly in our hearts for a lifetime.

In any battle the infantry is the heart and soul of the action. What those mud-Marines go through is both horrific and challenging, never to be forgotten by artillery, air, engineers, and tanks. Benis Frank said it well:

> Ground assault operations . . . were the special province of the armored and infantry units. Concerning the armored support of his 6th Division Marines, General Shepherd wrote, "If any one *supporting* arm can be singled out as having contributed more than any others during the progress of the campaign the tank would certainly be selected." In a battle lesson issued to his 32nd Army, Ushijima supported this theme, stating that "The enemy's power lies in his tanks. It has become obvious that our general battle against the American forces is a battle against their tanks."*

---

* *Okinawa: Touchstone to Victory,* (Ballantine, 1969), p. 158.

One of my regrets is to not have covered the battle for Kunishi Ridge on Okinawa more extensively. That would include strategic Hill 69 that flanked and defended Kunishi. The awesome price paid by all the depleted infantry regiments—First, Fifth, Seventh—at the ridge deserves the adulation of our nation.

At the time I was involved in the battle for Kunishi, I knew few infantrymen personally but witnessed their deeds of valor first-hand. In reunions and gatherings I've met Thompson Hargraves, Charlie Leonard, Bryan Downey, Brock Brockinton, and many others. I salute them all and their indescribable deeds.

In the taking of Kunishi Ridge, we tankers did some innovative things besides just destroying the enemy. We hauled up troops inside our tanks—also hauled up ammo, food, and water—to our precariously held foothold on the ridge. We hauled out many wounded on the backs and insides, acting as ambulance tanks. All the above deserves extensive coverage.

This book is not just about tankers, of course, but some wonder what is involved in being a tanker. In Chapter 24, Col. Walter "MuMu" Moore has given one of the best descriptions of tanks and tankers in combat that I have ever read. Tankers do more than just operate a steel monster.

Significantly of the five men in our C Company, First Tank Battalion, who were decorated—one Navy Cross and four Silver Stars—all were helping the wounded on their own initiative outside their tanks, on the back, or on the ground. Several were wounded in the process. In this book, I have included several of their citations. Howie Perrault, in Chapter 22, also courageously left his own tank to help rescue Ed De Mar. Unforgettable men with hearts of steel.

OKINAWA: THE LAST BATTLE

Introduction by Walter "MuMu" Moore

W orld War II ended fifty-three years ago! Sadly, to many it is
a faded memory. On the contrary, the men who fought and
died back then should never be forgotten. Readers of this book
will find it inspirational. Its pages tell a story of fighting men and
their experiences in adversity, heroism, forgiveness, and devotion.

The author could not have selected a better title. Appropriately enough, it fits the author's life perfectly, whether he intended
it or not.

Bob Boardman and I crossed paths when I joined Charlie
Company's First Tank Battalion on Pavuvu, Solomon Islands, in
1944. As Charlie Company's executive officer, it didn't take me
long to spot Corporal Boardman, the platoon commander's tank
driver (an important post!), as a "rock of stability and respect."
Not only in second Platoon but in the entire company.

Bob was more than a tank crewman; he also served as Charlie
Company's unofficial Chaplain, reaching out to men who needed
spiritual help. He was quick with a much-needed prayer in times
of battle stress. Don't get any ideas that this kind and gentle man
was some sort of namby pamby. Far from it. As in the case of Joshua
in the Old Testament, this ex-lumberjack and fighting Marine was
absolutely fearless in combat. This was attested to on countless
occasions during the battle for Okinawa.

This section contains a chapter titled "The Father's Day Massacre, June 17, 1945." It is a personal account described by several of
the veterans of this sanguinary day: Cpl. Bob Boardman, Lt. Jerry
"Ack Ack" Atkinson, Cpl. "Pop" Christensen, Sergeant Brenkert,

167

Pvt. K. C. Smith, and others whose lives were turned inside out that day.

Boardman, Brenkert, Bahde, and Alvarez all earned the Silver Star for "conspicuous gallantry in action." As a witness, I had the honor of writing the citations for these intrepid men. Indeed, they were all unforgettable men in unforgettable times. Semper Fidelis Marines!

WALTER "MUMU" MOORE
Former Commanding Officer and Executive Officer, C Company,
First Tank Battalion

TWENTY-ONE

SHERMAN TANK RAMS U.S. DESTROYER

Commitment beyond the Call of Duty

In Warfare, whatever can go wrong, will go wrong; whatever cannot go wrong, will also go wrong.

—*Anonymous*

This phenomenal event has happened only once in the annals of World War II and, for that matter, only once in the history of modern warfare as far as we know. For the invasion of Okinawa on 1 April 1945, the US Tenth Army under the command of Lt. Gen. Simon Bolivar Buckner, planned to land three Army divisions and two Marine divisions abreast on the East China Sea side.

In addition, the Twenty-Seventh Army and Second Marine Divisions were in floating reserve. The Second would make a feint landing on the southeast coast of the island at Minatoga Beach. This would hopefully draw large forces of the Thirty-Second Japanese Imperial Army defenders away from the real landing area at Hagushi beach.

D. I. Bahde, my close buddy, US destroyer rammer first-class, and I were in C Company, First Tank Battalion, First Marine Division. We were part of the initial assault force of 182,000 men. We knew the invasion force was huge, but didn't realize that it was 75,000 more men than had landed on D-Day at Normandy in 1944.

To our amazement and to that of every member of the landing force on Okinawa, the American assault from the sea was virtually unopposed. Total Tenth Army casualties were only twenty-eight

169

dead, 104 wounded, and twenty-seven missing. The first dead man I saw on the beach was a Navy frogman clad only in swim suit, flippers, and goggles.

Lt. Gen. Mitsuru Ushijima, commander of the Thirty-Second Imperial Japanese Army, in strategic consultation with Imperial Headquarters in Tokyo chose to offer only token resistance on the landing beaches and instead wage a prolonged war of attrition. He opted to utilize the natural coral-limestone ridges running east and west across the southern one-third of the island.

For months before the landing, Ushijima had his approximately 117,000-man force, which included conscripted Okinawans, dig with pick and shovel. They honeycombed the escarpments, ridges, and hills into veritable underground villages with amazing interlocking fields of fire against the enemy. These diggers lived the lives of moles and did not use any types of explosives to enhance their excavations.

The main Shuri line of defense was several stories deep with air conditioning and the entire line stretched six miles across the island and could hold 70,000—the bulk of Ushijima's forces. It was a seemingly impregnable defense. The general's great hope, along with Tokyo's strategic planners, was that in this planned war of attrition on the ground against the invaders, the Imperial Navy, Naval Air and combined Army Air units would be able to sink the bulk of our Navy. This would cut off vital supplies to our ground forces and force our defeat.

Our First Marine Division had traveled from Pavuvu in the Solomon Islands to Okinawa, a 1,500-mile journey with only a brief stop offshore in the Ulithi Islands. We were not allowed to disembark. The First Tank Battalion traveled aboard slow moving LSTs—Landing Ship Tanks. For many of us in C Company, Okinawa would be our third campaign. Cape Gloucester, New Britain, and Peleliu had made us into seasoned veterans.

While back on Pavuvu, our training and staging area for both Peleliu and Okinawa, our C Company tanks underwent a novel experiment. The First and Second platoons were equipped with T-6 flotation devices so that we could be launched at sea off the invasion beach and propel ourselves into shore like an amphibious tractor-tank. Only we would have heavier armor and a 75mm cannon, plus machine guns.

The unsung heroes of C Company were the maintenance men who kept our thirty-ton steel monsters operating. They welded steel flotation pontoons all around the hull, rigged a temporary steering device and installed small bilge pumps. The power to move these thirty-three ton (fully loaded with ammo) Shermans through the saltwater came from the steel tracks turning as the gears were engaged. The tracks were fitted with special track connectors with cups extending out that served as mini paddles. All seams in the tank hull and turret where seawater could enter were waterproofed.

We experimented with these devices off the waters around Pavuvu, but never had we driven off the steep steel ramp of an LST into fathomless depths off the landing beaches of Okinawa. This was the real thing. Our LST held six tanks with these bulky, space-consuming pontoons. Each tank with the T-6 units attached attained an increase in length and weight. The length was forty-seven feet and weight approximately forty-five tons. The pontoons were of steel with buoyant material enclosed in plastic bags inside each. Two pontoons were in front and two pontoons to the rear with a narrow pontoon on each side. The rear pontoon was rigged with twin rudders which were operated by ropes controlled by the tank commander.

Each of us drivers were sealed in our compartments—*entombed* might be a better word. The other four members of each tank crew stood on the back of the tank while the tank was driven off the ramp. It was a tense and crucial moment; good for the driver's prayer life!

There were so many snafus in time of war that, looking back, one seriously wonders at times how we ever won. It was helpful that the enemy had his abundant share of snafus also. We hadn't even landed on Okinawa and the first foul-up was taking place. We were let off the LST one hour late and, according to one report, ten miles at sea!

We were beyond the line of ten Navy battleships that were bombarding the shore with their fourteen- and sixteen-inch guns! It took us about five hours to reach the beach.

D. I. Bahde, from Kearney, Nebraska, was a sergeant in the First platoon commanding the first tank off the ramp. This tall, lanky, broad-shouldered offspring of German ancestry and I came out of boot camp about the same time and went through infantry training together at Camp Elliott in San Diego. Then because our names both began with B, we were "volunteered" for tank school at Jacques Farm together with a bunch of other A's, B's, C's, and D's. It didn't matter that we both were well over six feet and the tanks of that day were "lights" and very small.

Fortunately for us, by the time the Peleliu and Okinawa campaigns took place we had medium M4A2 diesel Sherman tanks. Room to burn!

As we began to move like a herd of turtles in the general direction of the Hagushi landing beaches, as yet indistinguishable, about one hundred yards from the LST, Bahde, in the lead, met his match.

A US destroyer came churning through the waters on course for a collision. Surely it would give way to this intrepid Marine barely-above-the-water-line-Civil-War-like Monitor vessel. Somehow the US Navy didn't get the word and that tin can watched this Sherman preparing to ram it on the starboard side. I wonder what those swabbies thought? Did they sound General Quarters—or did they line the railings and sing, "Here come the seagoing gyrenes"?

As Bahde's tank knifed through the brine at a blinding one knot per hour, history was about to be made. With a resounding *clunk,* the Sherman broadsided the US destroyer and gave those swabbies a sea story they're no doubt still telling their grandchildren.

Here are D. I.'s own words about that unforgettable cruise:

We finally repaired the rope by tying a knot in it so we could steer again and continued our journey to shore. Then smoke began to billow from the tank's exhaust system as we neared shore. Shortly thereafter my driver hollered up that his feet were getting wet, so I ordered him out of the driver's compartment. I had this sinking feeling—and the sinking feeling was that *we* were sinking! The tank had run out of diesel fuel and the auxiliary gas generator had also run out of fuel. With no generator the batteries died, and the bilge pumps stopped, thus that sinking feeling!

I crawled into the commander's hatch and handed out a quart of bourbon and Planter's peanuts that we had stashed in the five-man life raft.

I hollered to one of the guys to inflate the life raft and climbed out of the tank. To my horror I saw the life raft drifting away. No one had secured it! All this time the tank was steadily sinking, but we had also gotten closer to shore. My driver swam after the life raft and retrieved it. By this time the tank sank in about fifteen to twenty feet of water. We were left hanging onto the life raft and finally were picked up by an Amtrac and taken to shore."

[Shore, sweet shore, at last—Bahde and his intrepid crew thought! Although they now didn't have a tank to operate, at least they wouldn't have to become seagoing Marines again. Wrong! Bahde goes on with his story.]

After reaching shore I soon met Lt. Col. "Jeb" Stuart, commander of the First Tank Battalion. He asked me if I had removed the firing pin from our 75mm gun. I was completely taken aback and replied, "No, sir," but wanting to say, "Are you crazy!"

In any event, I was ordered to return to the sunken tank and remove the firing pin. I believe, at the time, Colonel Stuart felt that if the tide went out and the tank was exposed, the Japanese could use our own gun against us. I rode out to the spot on an Amtrac with an officer and tried to remove the firing pin. After five diving attempts, clad only in my green skivvies, the officer realized that the only way I could remove the firing pin was to drown myself in the process. He said, "No more" and that he would report, "mission accomplished."

We got back to shore just in time for two Japanese Zero fighter planes to spot us and make a strafing run. No casualties.

The deadly seriousness of war is often offset by humorous incidents such as these. In fact, without the humor we might not make it through with our sanity intact. Suffering, death, and destruction were waiting ahead in this three-month-long battle. In one period, 11–20 May, the First Marine Division "would lose 200 Marines for every 100 yards advanced," according to one military writer.

We also had a tragic footnote to the virtually unopposed landing on Okinawa. One of our other C Company tanks, after crossing the reef barrier off the Hagushi beach, blew off their flotation pontoons in the shallow water. They proceeded to move through the calm surf toward the landing beach and very suddenly drove into a huge, hidden hole that swallowed up the tank. Perhaps it had been made by one of the giant naval shells during the pre-invasion bombardment.

Four of the five-man crew escaped from the submerged Sherman. The driver, fighting and clawing against the pressure of the torrent of in-rushing seawater, was unable to extricate himself and drowned.

The remaining tanks could not get on or through the reef. Bill Henahan swam to the reef, walked ashore, and talked a bulldozer operator into coming out on the reef. Henahan said, "We unwound the cable from the dozer's winch and hailed a passing LCVP, which towed the cable out to our tank commanded by Lt. Jerry Atkinson. The dozer winched us up onto the reef. We then drove across the reef to shore. The remaining tanks sailed into the Sixth Marine Division beach area and got to shore safely."

D. I. Bahde, and his veteran crew, after such an "auspicious" start, were soon given a replacement tank and went on to distinguish themselves in three months of action on Okinawa. Twice Bahde was offered an opportunity to attend Officer's Training

School. Both times, once at Jacques Farm and the other at the end of the battle of Okinawa, he declined.

One thing I know for sure after the battle of Okinawa: if D. I Bahde had not turned down officer's training and had gone on to receive his second lieutenant's bars, he would have become the number one officer in charge of ramming naval vessels in all of the Marine Corps!

THE SECRETARY OF THE NAVY
WASHINGTON

The President of the United States takes pleasure in presenting the SILVER STAR MEDAL to SERGEANT DONALD I. BAHDE, UNITED STATES MARINE CORPS RESERVE, for service as set forth in the following CITATION:

"For conspicuous gallantry and intrepidity while serving as a Tank Commander of the First Tank Battalion, First Marine Division, in action against enemy Japanese forces on Okinawa, Ryukyu Islands, 22 May 1945. During an assault over difficult terrain, Sergeant Bahde was attempting to move his tank forward and destroy an enemy emplacement which had pinned down the accompanying infantry. When he observed two seriously wounded infantrymen lying in the path of his tank and unable to move, he promptly dismounted from his tank in the face of concentrated enemy fire and, crawling to the wounded men, carried them, one at a time, to the safety of his vehicle. Thereafter, he continued to advance and carry out his mission of destroying the enemy fortifications. His initiative, coolness under fire and unselfish devotion to duty were in keeping with the highest traditions of the United States Naval Service."

—JOHN L. SULLIVAN,
Secretary of the Navy for the President

TWENTY-TWO

SUGAR LOAF HILL

Greater Love Has No Man Than This

Courage is the first of human qualities because it is the quality which guarantees all others.

—*Winston Churchill*

The battle of Okinawa, 1 April to 21 June 1945, the last combat of World War II, cost the Americans, Japanese, and Okinawans a combined 230,000 dead. The names of all of these confirmed dead are inscribed on granite slabs in Peace Memorial Park at the southern tip of the island.

During that nearly three-month-long conflict, the American Tenth Army and the Japanese Thirty-Second Imperial Army fought a no-quarter battle, with Okinawan civilians caught in the middle. The Tenth Army was made up of four US Army divisions and three Marine divisions, the First and Second, both blooded units in previous Pacific battles, and the newly-formed Sixth Marine Division which was made up of a large nucleus of combat veterans from other units.

Of the 6th division's three infantry regiments, the Fourth Marines had the most tradition. The original Fourth Regiment had been lost in the Philippines at the beginning of the war; the regiment had subsequently been reconstituted around the former Marine Raider Battalions. A proud elite, the Raiders had seen much fighting at Tulagi, Guadalcanal, Bougainville and New Georgia before being formed into the Fourth Marines on Guadalcanal. *

* James H. Hallas, *Killing Ground on Okinawa* (Westport, CT: Praeger Publishers, 1996), 16.

The Twenty-Second Regiment had seen action on Eniwetok in the Marshall Islands and heavy fighting on Guam. The third regiment of the Sixth Division was the Twenty-Ninth formed at Camp Lejeune, North Carolina, in May 1944. It was made up of numerous veterans from Guadalcanal and Tarawa.

> The division's ranks included men of all types and backgrounds, from high-school dropouts to college graduates, from Depression-era dead-end kids to wealthy heirs, from bright-eyed young volunteers to skeptical draftees. Large numbers were still in their teens; few of the others were past their early twenties. "They called you 'Pops' if you were 26 or 27," recalled PFC Floyd Enman. *

A fateful destiny awaited many of these men on an unknown, inconspicuous hill not too far away as the Sixth Division moved south. Uncommon courage would become a common virtue.

Patrols of the Sixth Marine Division first came up against a "prominent hill" in front of the main Japanese Shuri Line of defense. A few days later the Marines named that hill Sugar Loaf. The battle for this one-hundred-sixty-five-feet-high by three-hundred-yard-long mound was anything but sweet!

According to one eminent military historian, *"there took place a combat not exceeded for closeness and desperation"* in World War II. In eight days of intense fighting Sugar Loaf changed hands at least eleven times!

The Japanese knew that if Sugar Loaf fell it would be a main key victory over the Shuri Line and ultimately all of Okinawa, so they desperately reinforced the hill with unit after fanatical unit. The toll on the enemy was as great and finally greater than that of the valiant Marine infantry and tankers, but the Marines had no way of knowing that in this fight to the death.

Four Marine infantry battalions melted away. Rifle companies all but vanished. With an original complement of 240, they

---

* James H. Hallas, *Killing Ground on Okinawa* (Westport, CT: Praeger Publishers, 1996), 17.

dwindled to twelve to twenty survivors. Eleven of eighteen company commanders were killed or wounded. Of four Sixth Division Medals of Honors awarded on Sugar Loaf, three were posthumous. Three thousand Marines were killed and seriously wounded. Another 1,289 were lost to sickness and combat exhaustion. The Sixth Marine Tank Battalion had thirty-three Sherman tanks knocked out in Hell's Half Acre, directly in front of Sugar Loaf.

I was in C Company First Tank Battalion, First Marine Division. We were heavily engaged on the left flank of the beleaguered Sixth, fighting through Wana Draw and Wana Ridge. As with most wars, we were deep into our own problems with the same tenacious enemy and had little or no knowledge of the difficulties and sickening losses on our right flank.

Who knows why the Sixth Division Marines named this hill Sugar Loaf. It was only and utterly bitter and poisonous to thousands of men of the Sixth. Perhaps it was the shape and color of this mound of death. Horseshoe Hill on the right and Crescent Hill on the left supplied interlocking fire along with devastating artillery, mortar, and rocket barrages that were zeroed in from the Shuri Line in the rear. Purple Hearts multiplied at a terrifying rate.

Cpl. Jim Day made it up Sugar Loaf on 14 May 1945, leading several other Marines to a shell crater where for three days and nights they fought off the continuous assaults of Japanese troops. Most of his mates were killed or wounded.

Day helped four wounded Marines, one by one to help and safety, but each time returned to clamber up Sugar Loaf. Finally only one wounded Marine remained with him in that precarious position. Wounded by shrapnel and burned by white phosphorus, Day held his ground. When finally relieved after those three harrowing days, enemy dead around his fighting hole were over one hundred.

Cpl. Jim Day made the Marine Corps a career and rose to become a major general. In over four decades and three wars, his valor in battle earned him a Bronze Star, three Silver Stars, and six Purple Hearts. His commanders on Sugar Loaf who would have recommended him for the Medal of Honor were all killed. Finally, fifty-three years later on 20 January 1998, this selfless hero and devoted patriot was awarded the MOH in a special ceremony at the White House.

Marine Infantry and tankers fought together, died together, and helped rescue one another in that inferno. Many helplessly pinned down and wounded "mud Marines" were straddled by thirty-three ton Sherman tanks, the escape-hatch in the bottom dropped and the Marine lifted up into the hot, cramped, but relatively safe shelter of the tank. They were then evacuated to our own lines and a battalion aid station.

Platoon Sgt. Ed De Mar of G Company, Second Battalion, Twenty-Second Regiment, badly wounded and lying helpless on the battlefield was ministered to under fire by a Marine he didn't recognize. Howie Perrault was a driver in Able Company, Sixth Tank Battalion commanded by Capt. Phil Morell, a veteran combat officer. Tankers like Perrault and Phil Morell on Sugar Loaf helped save many of G Company's stricken men at the risk of their own lives.

A few minutes later, Perrault, now wounded himself, and De Mar were placed side by side on the back of another tank. As De Mar turned to speak to Howie, he watched helplessly and in horror as a burst of machine gun fire caught Perrault in the head and killed him. Today, Ed De Mar from New York, is an honorary tanker.

"Greater love has no man than this, that a man lay down his life for his friends" (John 15:13).

Howie Perrault's sacrifice of his life for Ed De Mar is the epitome of being a Marine—the ultimate Semper Fidelis spirit. This kind of selfless love and comradeship has been repeated throughout the history of the Corps in many wars. The Savior Jesus Christ gave His life for each of us on the Cross two thousands years ago that we who were grievously wounded by sin and helpless before a relentless and cruel enemy, Satan, might have courage, hope, forgiveness, and the gift of eternal life.

TWENTY-THREE

RAISE THE BANNER

Victory over the Enemy

Yet, Freedom! yet thy banner, torn, but flying,
Streams like the thunder-storm against the wind.

—Lord Byron

Formosa (now called Taiwan) was the original mission objective, but at Admiral Nimitz's recommendation, the invasion was changed to Okinawa to allow more rapid movement for the Allies toward the Japanese mainland. We who made the landing on 1 April 1945 expected the same kind of deadly Japanese reception as at Peleliu—an intensive, life-and-death struggle on the beaches. Instead, it was a relatively peaceful landing.

On L (Love) Day, the only dead man I saw on the beach was a Navy frogman. My outfit, C Company, First Tank Battalion, First Marine Division, lost our first tank while crossing the coral reef when the tank unexpectedly drove into an unseen naval shell hole, trapping and drowning the driver.

Lieutenant General Ushijima, commanding the Japanese Thirty-Second Army, had chosen to make the defense of Okinawa a long, costly, drawn out one, in contrast to the invasions of Tarawa, Guam, Saipan, Peleliu, and other island battles. Because Japan's overall supplies were short and little was left of their naval forces, he counted on a war of attrition. The general hoped that the Kamikaze (Divine Wind) Force would destroy our invasion fleet by suicide attacks, cutting off supplies, thus isolating the invading expeditionary force.

On shore, we were unaware of this strategy and watched in awe, the dogfights in the air and the Japanese Kamikaze, as plane after plane plunged into our vulnerable ships. The US Navy suffered tremendous casualties. Contrary to all casualty ratios in war, their killed in action—4,907—was higher than the number wounded, 4,824. They led all branches of the Armed Forces in the number killed off Okinawa. Shrapnel, from ship and shore antiaircraft batteries, fell out of the sky raining down upon us with deadly effect, causing several casualties.

As the US Tenth Army, which included the First and Sixth Marine Division (with the Second in reserve) and the Army's Seventh, Twenty-Seventh, Seventy-Seventh, and Ninety-Sixth divisions searched for Ushijima, they found him and his main forces on the southern third of Okinawa. In an almost three-month-long, no-quarter battle through rice terraces, deep ravines, steep natural escarpments, coral caves, and fortifications, Ushijima exacted over twenty thousand Marine casualties, killed and wounded. Total Tenth Army plus Navy killed were 12,281.

Practically all of Ushijima's 117,000-plus ground troops were eventually annihilated by the Tenth Army. These included not only crack regular Japanese troops, but also fanatical native Okinawan conscript outfits such as the 750-man Blood-and-Iron-for-the-Emperor-Duty-Unit and six hundred Okinawan student "volunteers." Well over 100,000 Okinawan civilians died.

The year 1995 was the fiftieth anniversary of that memorable last combat of World War II. I cannot effectively put into writing the impact that the Battle of Okinawa has had upon my entire lifetime or upon those of my comrades. Our lives were changed forever. We can never forget Okinawa, as well as Peleliu.

One of the great, humorous, but also tragic stories to come out of the Battle of Okinawa was the assault upon General Ushijima's central command post in the tunnels under the rubble of what had been the ancient Shuri Castle. This was the heart of the Japanese main line of resistance.

A Company First Battalion Fifth Marine Regiment of the First Marine Division was ordered to make the assault on 29 May 1945.

Led by Capt. Julian Dusenbury, they quickly and effectively captured Ushijima's headquarters, although the general, his staff, and the bulk of his surviving troops had escaped to the southern tip of the island. Later, he and Lieutenant General Cho would commit ritual *hara-kiri* to try to atone for the defeat (See Chapter Twenty-Five, the "Three Lieutenant Generals' Appointments with Death").

It is important in any battle to raise your own banner upon achieving a major objective. This signals to the enemy that a major victory has been attained and has a demoralizing effect upon him. It also gives your own side a tremendous visible boost in morale and *esprit-de-corps*. The famous flag raising on top of Iwo Jima's Mt. Suribachi had this positive effect. It has been reported that the flag's domination over the high ground was enough to stop the fighting for a moment as hundreds of young Marines paused to cheer.

Captain Dusenbury did not have an American flag in his helmet liner, but "just happened" instead to have a Confederate flag from his native South Carolina. He hoisted the Rebel banner over the remains of the castle for all to see. Later he was reprimanded for this cheeky act by the First Division Commanding General Pedro del Valle, but back into combat he went. I met Julian some months later in the Philadelphia Naval hospital where we were both patients. Tragically, he was paralyzed from the waist down from a Japanese gunshot wound in the stomach.

One of the Hebrew names of God is the Lord Our Banner. If we follow Him, as A Company followed Julian Dusenbury, He will lead us to victory over the enemy, over temptation and over sin. We who profess the name of Christian must hold Christ high as our Banner, our flag of victory, for all people to see. Raise Him high by good deeds, by unashamed words, and by exultation and praise.

"Thanks be to God who gives us the victory through our Lord Jesus Christ." (1 Cor. 15:57).

TWENTY-FOUR

THE FATHER'S DAY MASSACRE, 17, JUNE 1945

Blood, Guts, and Glory

Charlie Company tanks take it on the chin and give it back.
—An Action Report—
by Col. Walter "MuMu" Moore, USMC (Ret.)
former CO and XO of C Company, First Tank Battalion,
holder of the Purple Heart, two Silver Stars
and two Legions of Merit with Combat Victory through
three wars

It took a great deal of intestinal fortitude to be cooped up in a World War II M4A2 Sherman tank. In essence, it was a blind, vulnerable beast for the five-man crew: Tank Commander (TC), gunner, and loader in the turret with the driver and assistant driver down in the front part of the armored chassis. The poor ventilation, dust, noise, heat, and stink of diesel fuel inside this steel box was enough to try any man.

The TC is forever making use of his periscope and vision blocks surrounding his hatch and cupola. Sticking one's head out the hatch for a quick look was like Russian roulette, a one-way ticket to oblivion! It was a full-time job checking for his supporting infantry, the position of his other tanks and overcoming anxious chatter on air in order to use his radio/intercom. The tank driver is always alert to the intercom guidance of his TC, as he peers through the limited vision of a periscope picking his way along. The danger of mine fields, ditches, mechanical failures, thrown track, antitank guns, fanatical Japanese satchel-carrying suicide troops were all a constant menace.

The Setting

It was around 0800 that fateful morning on June 17, 1945. The sun was already bright and clear. Charlie Company Tanks, Second platoon, was led by 2nd Lt. Jerry "Ack Ack" Atkinson and the Third platoon led by 1st Lt. Charlie Nelson had a total of seven tanks supporting Lt. Col. Hunter Hurst's Third Battalion, Seventh Marines (Hurst died in 1997, a retired brigadier general, awarded Silver Star, Peleliu; Navy Cross, Okinawa; and Purple Heart).

Hurst's Battalion attacked south from Kunishi Ridge. Their objective was the left portion of Mezado Ridge some six hundred meters distance. The First Battalion Twenty-Second Marines was on their right flank. The valley in which the tanks and infantry were to traverse was a fairly open field, filled with clumps of dry sugar cane and ditches—all excellent hiding places for the Japanese infantry and their automatic weapons, mortars, artillery, and observation posts.

We knew from bitter experience that the enemy's top priority was to stop our tanks, no matter what! This valley of death was no different. We soon discovered that the Japanese had our tanks sighted in with their 47mm and 76mm antitank guns set up into kill zones, firing in some cases from the flank no more than one hundred meters away. Like fish in a barrel.

Lt. Jerry "Ack Ack" Atkinson Starts His Story

June Seventeenth is my annual memorial day. Why? Because I'm living on borrowed time.

Father's Day, a bright Sunday morning, fifty-three years ago, June 17, 1945. Thanks to the Japanese Army's determination to kill me, my body became a literal sieve . . . shot at least seven times. Initially by an antitank slug from a Japanese 76mm gun hitting my tank. Later the enemy used my body for target practice, shooting me at close range. During the attempt to rescue me, Charlie

Nelson's gunner mistakenly hit me in the hand with a burst of co-axial .30 caliber machine gun fire. The story, still etched deeply in my memory, goes like this:

My platoon was supporting Lt. Col. Hunter H. Hurst's 3/7, pushing south toward Mezado. My buddy Charlie Nelson's Third Platoon was covering our advance from the vicinity of Kunishi town on high ground behind us. Sgt. Robert "Bob" M. Bennett, a squared-away Marine, my acting platoon sergeant, filled in as my gunner. He voluntarily replaced "Wild Bill" Henahan, the regular gunner, for the day. The night before, Henahan burned both his hands with hot coffee he had made on an open fire. My tank crew consisted of Cpl. Bob Boardman, driver, and a raw-boned Nebraska farm boy, Pvt. K. C. Smith was my loader. I don't remember the name of my assistant driver.

After receiving the signal from the infantry, my tanks crossed the Line of Departure south of Kunishi town. We led the infantry attack across the cane fields. If I recall correctly, we had four tanks in a line. Two of mine and two C Company HQ's tanks attached. Moving along in third gear, I kept a wary eye on the piles of dried sugar cane and brush in the field. Past experience proved that the [Japanese] made skillful use of such cover to hide troops, suicide teams, Nanbu MGs, and antitank guns. About half way across I peered through my vision blocks checking the infantry's progress which was supposed to be coming behind me. I couldn't see them, so I stopped our tanks immediately.

Bitter experience taught us that it was fatal to outrun your infantry support. Another quick look confirmed that many of them were stuck in a ditch about two hundred yards behind. For good reason, too! Heavy enemy artillery, mortar and flat trajectory fire prevented them from keeping up. Part of this fire was landing on and around our tanks. I was on the left flank with the other tanks running in an irregular line. Sergeant Brenkert's tank was to my right. Suddenly, I heard someone yelling on the platoon SCR 508 talk channel with unintelligible expletives, "Damn . . . damn . . . they are killing us."

Sgt. Bud Brenkert Picks Up the Story at this Point

The only thing I can add to what you already know via Bob Boardman was that my tank was the first one struck by the anti-tank guns. We were about two lengths to the right and in front of Atkinson's tank. One shell went through the steel holding piece, which was part of the pontoon apparatus on the front of the tank. The second shell penetrated the left side of the tank under "Pop" Christensen's seat. It was fragments from that shell which killed Hoffman, my assistant driver. The third shell struck the side of the tank and traveled through one fuel cell, coming to rest inside the fuel cell on the right side. Later we found this armor-piercing slug when the mechanics repaired the tank.

The high pressure released when the shell hit the fuel cell caused the vaporized diesel to spew out in large white clouds. I mistakenly thought that my tank was on fire.

The Japanese then shifted their fire to Lieutenant Atkinson's tank, setting it on fire. We were unable to move our tank at first because the round that passed under the driver's seat had fouled the gearshift mechanism.

Fortunately, "Pop," my driver, was able to free it up and we moved our tank alongside of Atkinson's tank, using it as protection from the antitank fire. I told Chris to drop the escape hatch and we waited for five minutes or so for someone to appear from Atkinson's tank. When no one did, we revved up the engines several times, indicating that we were backing up.

Atkinson Continues His Story

Suddenly . . . *Blam!* . . . *Blam!* . . . *Blam!* . . . *Blam!* . . . *Blam!* Five 76mm slugs, fired in quick succession, penetrated the armor on the left side of my tank. The first one broke the left track and left front drive sprocket. One round passed behind, barely clipping my driver's, Boardman's, seat. The velocity was such that this 76mm AP slug continued on, passing through the other side. Another round went through the lower turret into the fighting compartment, just missing K. C. Smith, the loader. Steel splinters splattered about, leaving him with a huge bloody chin gash. The round continued its deadly path, passing under the 75mm gun mount, almost cutting Sergeant Bennett, my gunner, in two. He was perched against my knees. That same round which killed Bennett struck my left thigh, just three inches above the left knee, leaving my left leg hanging there, held by only some bone and sinew. This deadly slug continued its travels, punching another hole on its way out the other side. Another round went through the turret tearing up the fuel pressure hoses spraying K. C. Smith and me with diesel fuel.

As I understand it from others, the fourth steel AP slug penetrated the engine compartment, opening the fuel cell and wrecking the port side GM diesel engine. White smoke and what I thought smelled like steam filled the fighting compartment. It was time to bail out. I shook Sergeant Bennett! His lacerated lower torso made it obvious he was dead. I pulled myself up through the turret hatch and jumped to the ground . . . mangled left leg and all! My tank was on fire. My remaining crewmen escaped, too. Boardman went up through the driver's hatch and K. C. Smith came out via his loader's hatch. They quickly spotted me laying by the tank. K. C. reached down and put my left arm around his neck. Boardman grabbed my other arm and hand and they struggled to carry me to safety.

I told them to watch out since the [Japanese] were in the dried sugar cane around us. We went about fifty to seventy-five feet from our tank with K. C. and Boardman stumbling and dragging me. A sniper shot Boardman's index finger off. The bullet then traveled through his throat, through the back of my neck and then struck K. C. in the face. I felt Boardman drop me and I fell on my face on the ground as this rifle bullet knocked me out. When I came to, blood covered my face and right cheek. My right arm was useless because of nerve damage.

I found out later that K. C. Smith thought that Boardman and I were dead. For good reason, Boardman, with his throat shot out, fell to the ground too, a bloody mess like me.

I opened my eyes and saw about six or seven Japs pushing the sugar cane aside looking at me. I tried desperately to move my right arm to get my .45 caliber pistol, which was in my shoulder holster. I intended to shoot myself to avoid the Japs cutting me up! Peering through my right eye, I spotted a Jap trench nearby. I wanted to get out into open ground and wait hopefully for Charlie Nelson's tanks to "rev up" their engines and fire their coaxial MGs over me. In the interim, the Japs looked scared and ducked down in the clumps of sugar cane. I counted up to five and rolled over to the right into the trench . . . lucky for me, no one was there. This was when I was able to face Nelson's tanks. I then straightened up, putting the Japs to my back out of their sight.

I waved my left arm and hand to Charlie Nelson's tank. Sadly, Nelson's gunner thought I was a Jap, cutting down on me with his coaxial .30 caliber. MG with tracer bullets! One of the rounds went through my left hand. I thought: "I haven't got a chance . . . my own men are shooting at me!"

Desperate, I lifted my right leg, the only limb I had left that wasn't damaged. Luckily, Charlie saw my booted leg with the red ski socks.

Suddenly two Marine infantrymen came running down and rolled me onto a poncho. Although grateful, I was too far gone to hurt any more. Using it as a stretcher, these brave men picked me up and ran back to Charlie Nelson's tank with me and placed me on top of the engine compartment. Charlie carried me on the back of his tank to a forward CP where Jerry Jerue and MuMu Moore questioned me. I told him where the AT guns were located and from then on you guys finished them off.

Sgt. Brenkert Carries on with the Story

It was confusion, disorientation, death, and fire that prevailed out in that field. After a while, I took my tank and slowly limped back to the road at the southern base of Kunishi Ridge. As we approached the road, Christensen spotted Boardman in the field. He stopped the tank and helped Boardman climb onto the tank. We then proceeded to the top of the ridge where Jerue and MuMu Moore were located. We took Hoffman out of the tank and discovered that he was dead. Boardman, who was bleeding profusely, was given first aid. We put him on the back of my tank and proceeded down from the ridge and across the no-man's valley to our lines. In the middle of the valley my tank ran out of fuel. We transferred Boardman to an accompanying tank and took him from behind our lines to the Seventh Marines aid station.

Cpl. Glenn "Old Man" Christensen Picks up the Story

I recall that morning as if it were yesterday. I was still driving Sergeant Brenkert's tank. We were positioned in a ragged line to the right and slightly ahead of lieutenant Ack Ack, our platoon commander's tank. I found out later our tank company was supporting 3/7 in their attack south of Kunishi town to Mezado ridge. Our tank was about half way across the cane field, when the lieutenant ordered Brenkert to move back because extremely heavy Jap antitank and artillery fire was zeroing in on us. Seconds after hearing this "backup" order, our tank was hit. A 76mm AP round entered the sponson under my seat, hit my assistant driver, Pvt. Albert "Scuddley" Hoffman, under the arm. He groaned. Hoffman was hit bad and was losing a lot of blood. I stopped the tank and held his body up. Then, as ordered, I put the tank in reverse and started moving back. The purpose of this maneuver was to take advantage of the protection offered by the embankment at the base of Kunishi Ridge.

Suddenly, Lieutenant "Ack Ack" called our tank for help. They, too, were being clobbered by a rapid succession of AT rounds coming from our left flank. Evidently the same guns had shifted fire, wreaking havoc on them. Because I was too busy maneuvering our tank, I had one of my crewmen reach down from the turret to keep Hoffman propped up. Brenkert reported that Lieutenant Ack Ack's vehicle was on fire and to pull around and try to pick up the survivors.

Try as I might, I worked to shift the tank's transmission but it was stuck. After several exasperating moments, I pulled a piece of metal stuck in the linkage and put it in first gear. Seconds later, another AT round hit us on the left side entering the engine compartment cutting through the fuel cells. I stepped hard on the foot throttle and kept moving. Smoke permeated inside the tank, blinding and choking us. Taking a chance, I opened the hatch and steered the tank with my head out.

We soon pulled up along side Ack Ack's tank and dropped the escape hatch. It was a bad place because the Japs were still shooting at us. The AP slugs sounded like a freight train as they roared past us. I felt something wet and, looking down at my legs, I noticed that diesel fuel from the blown hoses was spewing all over under my feet. Diesel fuel was also dripping out of the open escape hatch onto the ground. I stuck my head down through the hole under our tank looking for Ack Ack's crew. Sadly, no one was waiting to crawl up to safety.

Brenkert told us through the intercom that he couldn't see anyone from the turret. I asked for permission to crawl out and look into Ack Ack's burning tank. I told Brenkert, "If anyone should, I will." He replied, "No, absolutely not!"

Time was wasting. So I closed my driver's hatch. We were blinded again with the smoke and fire. Another call came in asking Brenkert to search for the missing Ack Ack and his crew. I muttered under my breath "that if they wondered where he was, why the hell didn't they go find him!" Another call from Lt. Jerry Jerue, our company CO, came over the air, ordering our tank to immediately return to the base of Kunishi Ridge.

Brenkert appealed to me saying that it was up to me to "nurse our tank back." We were spewing diesel fuel, had a simmering engine compartment fire, and were in danger of running out of fuel and being stuck out on the battlefield. I opened up my hatch as it smoked up again. There was no time to lose. With Brenkert guiding me, I backed up facing the enemy direction of fire. In this position, once our tormentors were spotted, Brenkert and our gunner were ready to shoot back.

I wasted no time heading to the relative safety of the Ridge base. Just about that time Bob Boardman and K. C. Smith, separately hiding from the enemy, came out from behind some bushes and rocks. We picked them up and headed for medical help. Then as luck would have it our tank ran out of diesel fuel. Fortunately, another tank pulled up and picked us up, continuing our mission of mercy, getting our comrades to emergency medical attention. At the aid station, the real sad part was struggling to get Hoffman, our dead comrade, out of the assistant driver's hatch, wrapped into a poncho, and laid to rest. That's something I still think about.

Bob Boardman Discusses His Rescue

I owe my life to these men. I came out of the sugar cane field and stumbled onto a dirt road. Just behind it was part of Kunishi Ridge and our forward CP. In desperation, I took a short cut by climbing directly up this steep ridge. It was a bad choice. Because I was extremely weak from the loss of blood I managed just a few feet before giving up. Just then Bud Brenkert's tank came out of the cane field. It limped along, smoke emitting from the exhaust.

I could see that it was severely hit by AT fire. For this reason, Glen "Old Man" Christensen, at twenty-seven, the oldest man in the company, was driving with his head out of the tank hatch. Christensen spotted me, stopped, helped me on to the tank. He quickly told me that Albert "Scuddley" Hoffman lay slumped over dead inside the tank. I was placed on a stretcher on the back of Brenkert's tank and we took off looking for help.

We weren't out of trouble yet. It was necessary to travel through the sniper-infested "No-Man's Valley," to reach Itoman where 2/7 had its battalion aid station. Sniper and automatic weapons fire kept zipping over the tank. In a selfless act of courage Bud Brenkert left the relative safety of the tank turret, placing his body across mine shielding me from the enemy fire. About halfway across "No-Man's Valley," Brenkert's badly damaged tank finally broke down. Waiting out there exposed to enemy action caused some tense moments!

Fortunately, another C Company tank commanded by Sergeant Brantly pulled up and pulled us out of a tough situation. Brenkert and Christensen carried me in the stretcher over to Brantly's tank. The rest of the crew pulled Hoffman's body out of the assistant driver's seat, placing him next to me on the back of the rescue tank. Fortunately, the rest of the trip to the medical evacuation point was uneventful.

Weeks later, Lt. Jerry "Ack Ack" Atkinson, my platoon commander, and I had an unexpected reunion in the San Francisco Receiving Hospital. Another of God's miracles, since neither of us were certain the other was alive.

Postscripts—Atkinson's Post-Battle Recollections

I went through the medical evacuation chain to a rear medical aid station. Eventually, I ended up on an LST used as a temporary hospital ship. This well-deck space was lined with cots. Oddly enough, the corpsman who took care of me and I were the only people in this massive tank well-deck.

Was I so messed up that they figured I was dying? Maybe the doctors were right. After all, I had seven holes in my body. This corpsman cleaned me up, wiped the blood from my hair and face. I figure to this day that this man helped me stay alive. Believe it or not, I discovered that he lived in Nashville just a few blocks away from my home.

It took me eighteen months to physically recover from my ordeal. However, the recovery phase of my life is another story. Since then, there isn't a day that goes by that I don't thank God for my comrades and my life. I still carry the constant reminder—body scars, a limp, and "what ifs" in my mind. In retrospect, halting my platoon in the open field was a mistake! Obviously, we became sitting ducks.

The now-famous red ski socks are a story in themselves. They helped save my life. If Charlie Nelson hadn't spotted them as I lay dying in that field fifty-three years ago, I'd be just another grave marker today. As I vividly recall, I stole them! How? In mid-March, the day we left Pavuvu, I stole them from my buddy "MuMu" Moore's (C Company Executive Officer) footlocker. (MuMu says not true, that he gave them to me). So it does pay to steal now and then. Therefore, I must thank God for Walter Moore, Charles Nelson, and Robert Boardman.

Postscripts—Brenkert's Post-Battle Recollections

That was the last time I saw Boardman until he visited me in Michigan, two years later. At that time, when I shook hands with

Bob, I noticed part of his right index finger was missing. He told me that when he was wounded, he tried to get my attention as that finger was killing him with pain, but all I was paying attention to was his throat.

When I returned to the company area, they told me that Joe Alvarez, my best friend, was another victim of the Father's Day Massacre. In the melee that morning Joe was hit by rifle or machine gun fire. He'd been evacuated through the medical chain to the States. I didn't see Joe again until I visited him in Arizona in 1947.

Postscripts—MuMu Moore's Post-Battle Recollections

It took Lt. Jerry Atkinson eighteen months to recover from his grievous wounds. Jerry still lives in his hometown of Nashville. This dynamic seventy-seven-year old is a semi-retired part owner of one of the largest insurance firms in Tennessee. Jerry, the strong-willed "people person," still has fire in his belly. He served as the vice-mayor of Nashville for two terms and in the state legislature for several years. Atkinson earned the Navy Cross for action on Okinawa.

On another occasion Jerry jumped out of his tank, crossed an open fire-swept area several times to rescue two Marines being butchered by the Japanese. Sgt. Bud Brenkert is a retired lawyer in Michigan, living a quiet life. Glen "Old Man" Christensen is another hardy eight-one-year-old retiree living in the small town of St. Elmo, Minnesota.

Sgt. Robert "Bob" Boardman, the former lumberjack from Washington State, became a "born again Christian" in Australia in 1943, long before the expression was coined. He is another robust forceful individual. He also spent eighteen months in various Naval hospitals.

Boardman's postwar life is a story in itself. The six-foot, three-inch Boardman speaks with a raspy voice, a reminder of the bullet that cut his vocal cords that fateful day in Okinawa. To show forgiveness, he devoted much of his life as a missionary in Japan. In recent years, this persevering comrade continues to search for "needy" souls. Bob has also made several missionary trips to Mongolia and heretofore forbidden areas in eastern Asia. This distinguished gray-haired Marine is a familiar figure at First Marine Division reunions. He is also the chaplain of the Marine Corps Tankers Association.

Brenkert, "Pop" Christensen, and Boardman were veterans of three campaigns—Cape Gloucester, Peleliu, and Okinawa. Brenkert, Alvarez, and Boardman are winners of the Silver Star for gallantry in action. As a witness, I had the honor of writing the citations for these intrepid men. Indeed they were all "unforgettable men in unforgettable times."

The men of C Company stick together. Today they call each other every Father's Day to reminisce about the day they cheated death.

JOSEPH RAMON ALVAREZ'S SILVER STAR CITATION

For conspicuous gallantry and intrepidity in action against the enemy while serving as a gunner with a Marine tank battalion on OKINAWA SHIMA, RYUKYU ISLANDS, on 17 June 1945. While engaged in evacuating wounded Marines from forward of friendly lines to a battalion aid station, Sergeant ALVAREZ voluntarily, and with complete disregard for his own personal safety, rode in a precarious position on the back of his tank giving aid to the wounded men and protecting them with his body. Although wounded while thus exposing himself to enemy machine gun and sniper fire, he made several trips in this manner before having his own wounds treated. His heroism and devotion to duty were an inspiration to his fellow crewmen and were in keeping with the highest traditions of the United States Naval Service.

—*Roy S. Geiger*
Lieutenant General, US Marine Corps

TWENTY-FIVE

THREE LIEUTENANT GENERALS' APPOINTMENTS WITH DEATH

Death Is No Respecter of Persons

Every man must do two things alone; he must do his own believing and his own dying.

—*Martin Luther*

When it comes time to die, make sure all you have to do is die.

—*Jim Elliot*

Death is no respecter of persons. It is amazing, however, that in the Battle of Okinawa, the last land battle of World War II, the three top ranking generals of both sides all took the journey of no return. Usually such high-ranking officers, although not impervious to a visit from the Grim Reaper, are well protected from the violence of front-line action. All died within less than a week of one another and at the very end of that terrible, tragic struggle that claimed over 230,000 deaths on both sides, including civilians.

Lt. Gen. Simon Bolivar Buckner, US Army West Point graduate in 1908, soldiered for thirty-seven years. He commanded the 155,000 ground troops of the American Tenth Army on Okinawa. This included the First and Sixth Marine Divisions with the Second in reserve, plus four US Army divisions—Seventh, Twenty-Seventh, Seventy-Seventh, and Ninety-Sixth. Buckner's violent death on 18 June 1945, three days before the island was officially declared secure, made him the highest ranking American to be killed in action in World War II.

A few days after General Buckner's death, on the very southern tip of Okinawa, as American troops closed in on their last command cave, Lt. Gen. Mitsuru Ushijima, commander of the defending Japanese Thirty-Second Army and his chief of staff, Lt. Gen. Isamu Cho, took their own lives by *hara-kiri* suicide.

Gen. "Buck" Buckner, age 58, a large, physically tough officer, was the epitome of an Army commander with his white hair and handsome good looks. He was an excellent student and teacher of battle strategy and tactics and had led the US campaign in the Aleutian Islands in 1943. He was decorated for ""exceptionally distinguished and meritorious service" and was basically an infantryman with special skill in tanks.

The general, however, was not without controversy: "He was not known as a man who liked to take risks; his instinct was to grind forward with the relentless use of superior firepower."

Several high-ranking Navy, Marine, and Army officers had recommended an amphibious landing to the rear of the fortress-like Shuri Line. This, hopefully, would help alleviate the purely frontal assault. Commandant of the Marine Corps and Medal of Honor recipient, A. A. Vandergrift, recommended using the Second Marine Division now waiting in reserve on Saipan. General Buckner turned down all recommendations.

> The absence of a landing [by the Americans] puzzled the Thirty-Second Army staff, particularly after the beginning of May when it became impossible to put up more than a token resistance in the south. *
> —*Colonel Yahara to US interrogators after the war*

After almost three months of no-quarter fighting, Buckner's Tenth Army had gradually driven Ushijima's exhausted, tattered, but brave remnants of the Thirty-Second Army to the southern

---

* James H. Hallas, *Killing Ground on Okinawa* (Westport, CT: Praeger Publishers, 1996), 17.

end of Okinawa. The Japanese still managed in the final weeks to extract about three thousand American casualties per week.

> The end of the battle on Okinawa was described in morale-building stories back home had almost nothing in common with how it appeared to sweaty US infantrymen, who knew each grueling, terrifying day might be their last."*

Buckner, who had described to newsmen the final operation as "mopping up," elected, against the advice of his staff, to visit a forward area to see for himself. On the afternoon of 18 June, accompanied by high ranking officers, he arrived at a forward observation post of an element of the Eighth Marine Regiment of the Second Marine Division, freshly arrived from Saipan.

In a few days with the island secured, the victorious general would report back to the US. No doubt he was, as a key general, in line for leadership in the coming invasion of the Japan mainland in the fall. But June 18, unknown to him, was his appointment with death.

The Marine forward observation post could see the cliffs and beach at the southwestern tip of the seventy-five-mile long island. The general was positioned between two large boulders about a yard apart and was handed a pair of artillery spotter glasses. All seemed so secure and safe.

The Japanese First Heavy Field Artillery Regiment, pride of the Thirty-Second Army, had only one gun left out of twelve. Their spotter, looking through his binoculars, saw what appeared to be a number of high-ranking officers. After one hour of viewing the battleground, Buckner confidently prepared to depart to visit another unit. At this moment the expert Japanese artillery officer gave word to fire and laid five scarce, precious rounds into this tempting target.

General Buckner's appointment with death had arrived. One of those five shells hit one of the boulders, showering chips, flying shrapnel, and coral fragments, some of which dug into the general's

---

* Feifer, *Tennozan* (New York: Ticknor & Fields, 1992), 502.

chest and abdomen. The profuse bleeding could not be stanched and in ten minutes he was dead.

> With so much death everywhere, his seemed to some "not inappropriate." And it was a matter of inches, in the battlefield way. None of the officers accompanying him were scratched. Like so many of his men, the commander had been dealt a dose of combat's vast store of random bad luck. *

The deaths of Lieutenant Generals Ushijima and Cho were very different from that of the American commander. They chose their own path or means of traveling into eternity. Their last command cave was only about one mile south of the spot where General Buckner met his fate.

The two Japanese generals had gradually withdrawn the Thirty-Second Army from much of the almost impregnable Shuri Line during the period of May 22–31 in order to make their prolonged, but hopeless last stand in southern Okinawa. Their final command cave was a far cry from their former headquarters beneath the rubble of Shuri Castle.

The underground Shuri complex was about 1,300 feet long with tiered levels and blower-assisted ventilator shafts. The entire Shuri Line fortification running several miles across Okinawa, with interconnecting tunnels, could hold the great bulk of the seventy thousand defending troops.

Now their relatively small cave, inside of Hill 89 to the Americans, near the village of Mabuni, was the scene of their final orders and a farewell party for their staff. General Ushijima, in full dress uniform, challenged the survivors present "to fight to the last and die for the eternal cause of loyalty to the Emperor." Cho wore a white suicide ceremonial kimono. With their staff they dined well and toasted one another with Black and White Scotch whiskey carefully transported from Shuri. Then they sang "Umi Yukaba," an ancient drinking song that had become like a national anthem to the Japanese.

---

* Feifer, *Tennozan* (New York: Ticknor & Fields, 1992), 504.

These were the modern Samurai commanders who had attempted to instill into all their defending troops the following resolute battle watchword:

> One plane for one warship.
> One boat for one ship.
> One man for ten of the enemy or one tank.

As dawn approached on 23 June and as units of the US Army Seventh Division overran Hill 89, the generals and remnants of their staff made their way to a narrow ledge outside the cave overlooking the ocean two hundred feet below. As they stepped outside the cave Lieutenant General Cho turned to his superior: "Well, Commanding General Ushijima, as the way may be dark, I, Cho, will lead the way to the outside ledge." Ushijima replied, "Please do so. I'll take along my fan since it's getting warm."

Even as the Americans closed in lobbing grenades toward the movement of the Japanese below on the ledge, James and William Belote recount the last moments of the two generals:

> Both knelt on the sheet, facing the ocean since room was lacking on the ledge to perform the ceremony facing north toward the Imperial Palace. Silently each opened his tunic, baring his abdomen. At General Ushijima's side stood his aide, Lieutenant Yoshino, holding two knives with half the blade wrapped in white cloth. The adjutant, Captain Sakaguchi, stood on Ushijima's right, saber drawn. Yoshino handed a blade to Ushijima, who took it with both hands and, with a shout, thrust. Simultaneously, Sakaguchi's saber fell on his neck as prescribed, severing his spinal column. Ushijima's corpse lurched forward onto the sheet. Then General Cho took his turn and the ceremony was repeated.*

That is how most accounts tell the story of these two generals' final earthly moments. There is, however, controversy even over the final date, because of conflicting reports. Perhaps all of this is

---

* Feifer, *Tennozan* (New York: Ticknor & Fields, 1992), 507.

the romanticized version for the Japanese public. Likely we will never know.

The seven or nine Japanese staff officers, who witnessed and assisted the generals' final moments, all reportedly killed themselves with a bullet to the head immediately following the burial of the commanders. A year following Ushijima's death, the Japanese government promoted him posthumously to General of the Army. This seems strange and even bizarre not only to us Westerners, but also to certain Japanese. Especially when tens of thousands of Okinawan civilians needlessly died in this deadly conflict.

One of the surviving Japanese soldiers of Okinawan birth from the battle of Okinawa, upon reflection after the war, may have summed up the two Japanese generals' responsibility best:

> The commanders of the Okinawa Defense Forces ended their lives as warriors but could not escape criticism for dragging not only their fine soldiers, but also the unfortunate civilians into the war. It did not matter to others that they had acted "under orders."
>
> —*Masahide Ota*

Okinawa. D. I. Bahde's flotation tank after ramming US Destroyer. Note the billowing smoke and steam. Chapter 21.

Okinawa. Evacuating the wounded near Sugar Loaf Hill along narrow gauge railway. Chapter 22.

Okinawa. C Company, First Tank Battalion tank which carried wounded
Pvt. W. D. Fuhlrodt from Kunishi Ridge to Battalion Aid Station.

Okinawa. C Company tank and officers behind the front lines about 16 June 1945. L to Are: Lt. Tom Duddleson, Fourth Plt, deceased; Lt. Kessler, First Plt; Lt. Charlie Nelson, Third Plt., deceased; Lt. Jerry Jerue, CO, C Company, deceased; Lt. Walter "MuMu" Moore.

Muscle Men of C Company, First Tank Battalion, after the battle of Okinawa, Survivors of the 2nd Platoon. Front row left, Olie Olson, Hoover, Soltinski, Payne, Rybaski. Standing L to R are: Giordino, Don Thompson, Bud Brenkert, Printz, Old Man Christensen, K.C. Smith. Missing from the picture: John Moore and Roy Herschberger.

Okinawa. First Marine Division cemetery. Olie Olson kneeling by grave of Robert Bennett, killed in our tank. Chapters 1 and 24.

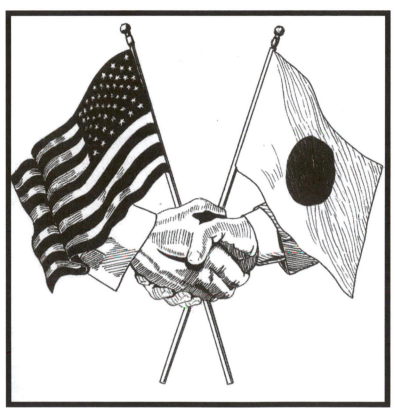

VI. RECONCILIATIONS AND
RETURNS TO THE
BATLEFIELDS

TWENTY-SIX

I COULD NOT FORGIVE UNTIL

Dealing with Unforgiveness

A wise man will make haste to forgive, because he knows the full value of time and will not suffer it to pass away in unnecessary pain.

—*Rambler*

Perhaps the most difficult thing in the world is to say to someone who has not asked for your forgiveness, "I forgive you," and mean it. It is easier to carry around a spirit of bitterness and unforgiveness, although in the long run, that bitterness will eventually eat us up and kill our own spirit. It is a venomous, infectious poison.

Unforgiveness can be a very subtle thing though. Sometimes we don't even realize it is present in our lives until it is challenged. I personally had to learn forgiveness of the Japanese the hard way. During the last land battle of World War II, our invasion of Okinawa, I had been shot through the throat and hand, hospitalizing me for eighteen months. There were two men in my life who taught me and enabled me to give up a resentful spirit that I didn't realize I had until it was challenged.

The first man was plenty tough. Can you believe he was as tough as any Marine? He was Louie Zamperini of the old Army Air Corps. Zamperini ("Zamp") was a world-class runner and was ultimately chosen as a member of the All-American college team and participated in the Olympic games in Berlin. He wanted a Nazi flag for a

211

souvenir so shinnied up a fifty-foot flag pole and brought down the swastika, but came close to being shot for his antic. Hitler allowed him to keep the banner. After the Japanese attack on Pearl Harbor, December 7, 1941, Zamperini joined the Air Corps, was shot down in the Pacific and survived forty-seven days on a life raft.

The drifting raft ended up on the Japanese occupied island of Guam. When they landed, they were too weak to walk. He and the only other surviving crew member could only crawl ashore on their hands and knees. They were immediately captured by the Japanese and soon sent to a prison camp in Japan.

In prison when the guards learned Zamp had been a champion runner, they brutally beat and starved him. Fourteen days in a row, Sergeant Watanabe, nicknamed "The Bird" by the Allied prisoners of war, beat Zamp with his heavy web steel belt buckle, then made him compete in running events, though he then weighed less than one hundred pounds. If he lost, they beat him; if he won, they beat him harder.

Zamperini prayed to God for mercy on that life raft in the middle of the Pacific Ocean—and now in prison he renewed his prayer of repentance. God delivered him at the end of World War II, and he returned home and became an instant hero and a heavy drinker— and then he forgot God and his vows of service to God if his life would be spared.

I was in a large meeting in 1951 and heard Zamperini tell the above story. At the time I was going through my own personal struggle, for I knew God wanted me to be a missionary to Japan. I could not accept what I thought was a very unreasonable assignment from God. "Lord, I'm willing to go anywhere in the world, except Japan," I prayed. The memories of three bitter battles and the loss of many close buddies just wouldn't allow me to say, "Yes, Lord."

For many weeks I fought God and was miserable. I did not realize there was a residual feeling of bitterness within my heart until God indicated that He wanted me to go to Japan as His servant.

In that 1951 meeting, Louis Zamperini continued his story. He said:

When I forgot my promises to God in the clamor and excitement and false ambition of postwar living, I was worse than the prison guards in Japan who had beaten, starved, and tortured me, denying me the dignity of human treatment: for I had denied God in my search for notoriety and material gain.

Zamp finally repented from his willful, materialistic outlook, and rebelliousness and returned to Japan for a few months to share the Good News of Jesus Christ with the Japanese people. But his supreme test of faith was whether he could visit Sugamo Prison in Tokyo, come face to face with his former guards and say, *"I forgive you, in Christ's name."* God's mercy and grace dwelling within enabled him to do this.

When I heard Zamperini's story, all my own resistance broke down and I said "Yes" to God. The last day of 1951 I departed for Japan on a three-passenger freighter. Today, by God's goodness, many Japanese are among my best friends.

The second man I learned forgiveness from was brutalized by men far more than Louis Zamperini or any person who ever lived. He allowed the sins of you and me to be placed upon Him and died in our place as a loving, forgiving sacrifice that we might have life and hope beyond this earthly existence. He is Jesus Christ—more than a man—perfect God and perfect man.

In a simple, childlike act of faith, you and I can be forgiven, by accepting Him as our personal Savior. Forgiveness from Him enables us to forgive and love those we cannot even naturally like. Let His forgiveness flow into your life and erase your bitterness. Then forgiveness and love can flow through you reaching out to, what are to you, an unlovable person or people.

"Forgive them Father, for they know not what they do" (LUKE 23:34).

Here is an update on Louie Zamperini's amazing eighty-one-year-old zestful life. During the 1998 Winter Olympics he returned to Japan to carry the Olympic torch through the town of Naoetsu on the way to Nagano, headquarters of the Games. Naoetsu was the village where Zamp was imprisoned for most of those thirty months during the war.

The Japanese, and especially the townspeople of Naoetsu, honored and cheered this eighty-one-year-old American—and in a sense apologized to him for the brutality he suffered at their hands in World War II.

"The Bird" Watanabe still survives. Though now long retired, he became a prosperous businessman. After the war, the Allied War Crimes Tribunal searched for him to put him on trial for atrocities committed against Allied POWs. He successfully eluded capture. During the 1998 Winter Olympics CBS interviewed Watanabe. Louis Zamperini had an appointment to meet The Bird face to face, but The Bird broke the appointment.

What would Zamp have said to Watanabe if that meeting had happened? Simple: *"I forgive you and love you with Christ's love."*

TWENTY-SEVEN

TWO ENEMIES EMBRACE ONE GOD

From Pearl Harbor to Prison Camp,
Reconciliation with the Enemy

This is certain, that a man that studies revenge keeps his wounds green, which otherwise would heal and do well.
—*Francis Bacon*

Never were two men less likely to become reconciled than Mitsuo Fuchida and Jacob DeShazer. Their countries, Japan and America, were the world's largest ocean apart. Backgrounds, languages, customs, traditional religions, thinking patterns, physical makeups, philosophies of life—all were as different as those of any two peoples on earth.

By the end of World War II, the most extensive war man has ever known, nearly sixteen million Allied and Axis servicemen had died. Both Fuchida and DeShazer were fanatically determined to inflict a maximum number of casualties upon the other side, even at the cost of their own lives. As implacable enemies, the two men took part in two of the most dramatic events of the Pacific war. Fuchida led the attack on Pearl Harbor and DeShazer was one of the Doolittle raiders who made the first American bombing run on Japan.

How did Fuchida and DeShazer, young antagonists in the prime of life, come through the intense combat of World War II? Did they continue their bitter rivalry after the war? Or did they learn lessons in true living from their sufferings and defeats? Did they perhaps learn how to pray—to call out in sincerity to a God greater than their own limited and weak resources?

Mitsuo Fuchida

Mitsuo Fuchida was born in 1902, the quiet son of a school principal, in a small village outside of Osaka, Japan. He eventually became a pilot in the Imperial Japanese Navy. His diminutive physical makeup belied the tough character of the inner man. He became one of his navy's top flyers. By attack time on Pearl Harbor, he was a veteran of the Sino-Japanese War, having logged three thousand hours of flying time. Because of his outstanding leadership abilities as well as flying skills, he was the unanimous choice as flight commander of the 360 planes that smashed Pearl Harbor.

Adm. Isoroku Yamamoto, the overall planner and organizer of the attack, handpicked Fuchida to lead the attack from the Japanese Pearl Harbor Carrier Striking Force (*Kido Butai*). This formidable armada, which sailed from Japan's Inland Sea on 16 November 1941, consisted of six aircraft carriers, two fast battleships, two heavy cruisers, one light cruiser, eight destroyers, three oilers, and a supply ship. The original Pearl Harbor attack plan called for this to be a one-way mission by the pilots. That plan was dramatically changed when some of the flight squadron commanders, upon learning of it, threatened to personally kill those planners. *

The mighty armada of 360 planes took off at dawn for the surprise attack on America's mightiest naval base. Fuchida arrived over the island of Oahu to approach Pearl Harbor in his light, high-level command bomber on Sunday, December 7, 1941, American time. It was December 8th in Japan. At exactly 7:49 a.m., he gave the code word *Totsugeki* (Charge!).

The lead attack planes peeled off to attack. After a few minutes, Fuchida set off a blue flare to signal the other planes that complete surprise had been achieved. Next he radioed Vice Admiral Nagumo, *"Tora, Tora, Tora!"* (Tiger, Tiger, Tiger!). This was the

---

* John Toland, *Rising Sun*, Vol. 1 (New York: Random House, 1970), 214.

code for "We have succeeded in surprise attack." Wave after wave of torpedo planes, dive bombers, high level bombers, and zero fighter planes devastated the peaceful Sunday routine of Americans in and around Pearl Harbor, Hickam Airfield, and Wheeler Airfield.

> At Pearl Harbor it was confirmed that eighteen ships had been sunk or badly damaged; 188 planes destroyed and 159 damaged; 2,403 Americans killed. It was a disaster but it could have been a catastrophe. Luckily, the carriers were at sea and the enemy had neglected to bomb the oil storage tanks at the Navy Yard and the submarine pens. Moreover, almost all of the sunk or damaged ships would eventually return to battle. The Japanese lost 29 planes and five midget submarines; forty-five airmen had died, and nine submariners. One, Ensign Sukamaki, was captured when his boat went aground on the other side of Oahu. *

As a result of this surprise attack, Fuchida became a national hero. Later, along with Vice Admiral Nagumo, he was ordered back to Tokyo to make a personal report before the Emperor of Japan. Because the Japanese people considered Hirohito divine, a direct descendant of the sun goddess, it was an awesome event for Fuchida to appear before the throne. He was not supposed to speak to the emperor directly, but rather through an imperial aide. However, Fuchida became so flustered that he replied to the emperor, and later confessed that this experience was worse than the attack on Pearl Harbor!

By the end of the war, almost all of Fuchida's flying comrades had been killed in combat. He was at the battle of Midway, a turning point in the war in favor of the Allies. There, Japan lost four aircraft carriers, many planes and choice pilots. Fuchida was to lead the attack on Midway Island, but came down with a sudden attack of appendicitis and ended up in the sickbay aboard his carrier, Akagi, completely frustrated. That sickness no doubt spared his life.

---

* John Toland, *Rising Sun*, Vol. 1 (New York: Random House, 1970), 295.

Miraculously, time after time throughout the war, while others were dying all around him, his life was preserved. One can only conclude that God had a special destiny for Mitsuo Fuchida. Yet the eyes of his spiritual understanding would not be opened to God's plan until many months after the war.

Jake DeShazer

In the meantime, the United States felt an urgent need to strike a physical and psychological blow at the Japanese that would let them know what was coming. What better message than to bomb the Japanese homeland? The US Navy devised an ingenious plan for medium-sized American bombers to take off from a Navy aircraft carrier, fly five hundred miles to the Japanese mainland, drop their bombs, and then crash-land in China.

Lt. Col. James H. Doolittle, aeronautical scientist and skilled pilot, was chosen to lead this daring raid. He had already been commended for many speed records and firsts: He was the first pilot to cross the United States in twelve hours, first to do the almost-impossible outside loop, and first to land an airplane by instruments alone. Since it would be an extremely hazardous mission in which some pilots would surely die, volunteers were called upon to man the sixteen crews. The preparation and training would not only be intense, but also highly secretive.

Jacob "Jake" DeShazer was already in the Army Air Corps at the time of the attack on Pearl Harbor and his reaction was instant: "As I heard the news my heart was filled with hatred and revenge. It seemed like a sneak attack. One month later, I volunteered for the mission with Jimmy Doolittle . . . "*

Jake was born in Salem, Oregon, on November 15, 1912. His father died when he was two years old, and soon afterward his mother remarried. Jake recounts his early life:

> My stepfather had a big wheat ranch and he was a very godly
> man. He used to pray every morning and read the Bible with tears

---

* Jacob DeShazer, *Fuchida Remembered* (Tokyo: Japan Harvest, 1975), 18.

coming from his eyes as he prayed. But, when I got to be nineteen years old, I rejected the teaching of my parents. I felt at that time Christianity was like any other religion. I did not know who Jesus was. I went out to get a job, but it was Depression time so finally I ended up in the United States military service as an airplane mechanic. I was working on the B-25s at the time Pearl Harbor was bombed. I also was taking training to be a bombardier. *

Jake, like so many American young people, was born of Christian parents and raised in an atmosphere of the church, but was without a personal encounter with Jesus Christ. He was living on the fruit of the gospel, but it had never become a part of his life. He was still as far from forgiveness of his sins and repentance as was his avowed enemy, Mitsuo Fuchida. In order for DeShazer to have a change of heart and turn to God, it would take forty terrible months of imprisonment to soften and prepare his hard, hate-filled heart. All but 185 days of that time would be spent in solitary confinement.

The takeoff on 18 April 1942, of the sixteen overloaded, modified B-25s from the aircraft carrier *Hornet*, five hundred miles from the Japanese mainland, was a dramatic event. Lieutenant Colonel Doolittle's lead plane had only 467 feet of runway on the carrier deck. With throttle wide open, the nose lifted off with just a few yards to spare. Jake was bombardier on the last plane. A seaman on deck lost his footing and was blown into one of the spinning propellers of Jake's plane, mangling his left arm. This unnerved the pilot, who pulled a control lever the wrong way. The plane shot off the bow, dipped, and disappeared from sight of the ship. In a few moments the plane regained both control and altitude, skimming across the waves to join the other fifteen planes winging toward Japan.

Each of the thirteen planes dropped its cargo of four bombs on Tokyo. The other three planes bombed the major cities of Nagoya, Osaka, and Kobe. The surprise was as complete as the Japanese attack on Pearl Harbor, although the damage was not nearly as

---

* Charles Hembree, *From Pearl Harbor to the Pulpit* (Akron, OH: R. Humbard), 95.

extensive. All the pilots of the planes completed their mission, and then continued on to either crash-land or bail out in China—all except one, who landed safely in Eastern Russia.

> The other fifteen bombers came down in Japanese-occupied China. Three men were killed in crash landings or bailouts; eight were captured and bought to Tokyo for trial. The rest, including Doolittle, were alive and heading by various routes for Chiang Kai-Shek's lines. *

Jacob DeShazer was one of the eight captured. All were given death sentences. Three of the eight were executed immediately because of the anger of the Japanese over the bombing. The emperor eventually commuted the death sentences of the remaining five, although they were in torturous suspense about their fate for many months. After trials in Tokyo, the five were returned to prison in China, where they served most of their forty months.

In their prison in Shanghai, China, the men went through the ordeal of overcrowded cells, a small receptacle used for a toilet for fifteen people, boiled rice soup for breakfast, and four ounces of bread for both lunch and dinner. There were bedbugs, lice, and large rats freely scurrying around their cell. In winter it was bitter cold, and in summer the weather was sweltering. The men were put on a starvation diet for almost twenty months. DeShazer came to the lowest point of his life. He recalls:

> In the daytime we had to sit straight up on the floor without any support for our backs. Often the guards caught us leaning back on our elbows, and hit us sharply on the head with a bamboo stick. One of the most painful torture methods our captors used was making us kneel for hours on a sharp-edged board. They had formed a triangular board with the razor-sharp edge up. We were forced to kneel on this edge for hours on end. Of course the sharp edge would cut into our knees until we could hardly walk.†

---

* John Toland, *Rising Sun*, Vol. 1 (New York: Random House, 1970), 386.
† Charles Hembree, *From Pearl Harbor to the Pulpit*, 37.

On 1 December, Lieutenant Meder died from mistreatment. Jake and the other three surviving Americans were allowed to take one last look at Meder's body as it lay in a wooden box just before cremation. On top of the box lay a wreath of flowers and his Bible. Meder's death, when reported to higher Japanese authorities in Tokyo, brought better treatment for Jake and the others. Meder, a Christian, was like the proverbial grain of wheat falling into the ground and dying (John 12:24). Only then does it multiply its fruitfulness. His life, and now his death, had an impact on Jake, a close buddy:

> Lieutenant Meder seemed to understand the Bible well. He told me that Jesus Christ is the Lord and coming King. That Jesus is God's Son and that God expects the nations and people to recognize Jesus as Lord and Savior. I did not understand what he meant at the time, but I remembered his words later. It was after Meder's death that I began to ponder the cause of such hatred between members of the human race. I wondered what it was that made the Japanese hate the Americans, and what made me hate the Japanese. My thoughts turned toward what I had heard about Christianity changing hatred between human beings into real brotherly love, and I was gripped with a strange longing to examine the Christian's Bible to see if I could find the secret. I begged my captors to get a Bible for me. At last in the month of May 1944, a guard brought the Book, but told me I could have it for only three weeks. *

Eagerly, day and night, Jake read the Bible. As he came to Romans 10:9 on June 8, 1944, he confessed Christ with his mouth and believed in his heart that Jesus is the true Son of God and had been raised from the dead. As Jake pondered the words found in 1 John 1:9, he received assurance of his sins being forgiven:

> How my heart rejoiced in my newness of spiritual life, even though my body was suffering so terribly from the physical

---

* Charles Hembree, *From Pearl Harbor to the Pulpit*, 39.

beatings and lack of food. But suddenly I discovered that God had given me new spiritual eyes, and that when I looked at the Japanese officers and guards who had starved and beaten me and my companions so cruelly, I found my bitter hatred for them changed to loving pity. *

Jake goes on to tell of the dramatic impact that the reading of God's Word had upon his life:

I read in my Bible that while those who crucified Jesus on the cross had beaten Him and spit upon Him before He was nailed to the cross, He tenderly prayed in His moment of excruciating suffering, *"Father, forgive them; for they know not what they do."* And now from the depths of my heart, I, too, prayed for God to forgive my torturers, and I, determined by the aid of Christ to do my best to acquaint the Japanese people with the message of salvation, that they might become as other believing Christians. A year passed by and while the treatment did not change, I did. I began to love my captors.†

God used Lieutenant Meder's life and death to awaken Jake, but there was another source of power behind the scenes. This was a godly mother who did not cease to pray for her son. She says:

My story is not one of boastful pride, but of witness to the goodness of the God who ever hears and answers the intercessory, pleading prayers of a Christian mother. My son, Jacob DeShazer, is a loving example of what the Lord can do for any mother who really "gets hold of God" for the solving of every trial and problem in the rearing of sons and daughters.‡

---

* Charles Hembree, *From Pearl Harbor to the Pulpit,*40.
† Ibid., 40-41.
‡ Ibid., 43.

What debt do so many of us owe to behind-the-scenes godly mothers who "get hold of God" in prayer? Far more than any of us can imagine. Napoleon was once asked what France's greatest need was. He immediately replied, "Good mothers!"

In 1945, American paratroopers dropped into the prison compound in a dramatic and emotional rescue of the emaciated Doolittle survivors. In due time, Jake fully recovered. He attended Bible college in the United States, the first step of a vow he had made to return to the land of his former enemy as a missionary. During his college days, he met Florence, a wonderful young woman, whom he married.

Both Warriors Share the Open Secret with the Japanese

On 28 December 1948, Jake and Florence landed on the docks of Yokohama feeling apprehensive about how their former enemy would receive them. One Japanese girl vowed to kill Jake because she had lost her sweetheart in the Doolittle raid. However, she repented and became a believer during one of Jake's meetings. Because thousands of Japanese had lost loved ones during the war, many of them held a deep-seated enmity toward Americans.

In the immediate postwar years, God mightily used the story of Jake and Florence DeShazer throughout Japan to help reconcile the former enemies to one another and many Japanese people to the Great Reconciler. In one of Jake's public meetings in Osaka, four years after his return, two of his former prison guards became believers when they heard his testimony. What drama and emotion there was in that encounter! Could there ever be any more dramatic account of reconciliation? The answer was to be *yes* when we see what happened in the life of Fuchida. Mitsuo Fuchida came back from losing the war a miserable, dejected man. Most of his flying companions were dead. Japan had been devastated by the Allied bombings, and his people were defeated and discouraged. Many had lost all their possessions and were close to starvation. Never in Japan's history had foreigners occupied her land. Now all that had changed. What hope was there? Here are Fuchida's own words:

> From Pearl Harbor day I spent myself as a most patriotic soldier for my mother country. But four years later, Japan had lost the war. I returned to Nara Prefecture disillusioned and took up farming. These were the most miserable days of my life.
>
> However, one day General MacArthur, the supreme commanding officer of the occupied forces, asked me to come to Tokyo to testify at the war trials. I got off my train at the Shibuya railroad station and there I saw an American handing out leaflets. When I passed by him, he gave me one. I saw this pamphlet was the story of DeShazer. There was a startling title, *I Was a War Prisoner of Japan.*
>
> I never had read the Bible. At that time I was 47 years old and during all my life I had never heard the name of Jesus. I was very lost. Jake DeShazer's story inspired me to get a Bible. I bought a Bible and read through the pages so eagerly every day. One day as I was reading the Bible, I came to Luke 23:34. Jesus was hanging on the cross, nailed there, yet He prayed, *"Father, forgive them; for they know not what they do."* Right at that moment Jesus came into my heart.
>
> I clearly understood what Jesus had done on the cross. He died, too. Right away I accepted Him as my personal Savior. Then He transformed me. I was a sinner, but He cleansed me. Since then I dedicated the balance of my life to serving Him. *

Later Mitsuo Fuchida and Jake DeShazer met in a dramatic moment of full reconciliation: One-time enemies now worshipping and serving the same God, the Lord Jesus Christ. This was truly a miracle. Only the living God could cause such a transformation in the hearts and lives of avowed enemies.

---

* Charles Hembree, *From Pearl Harbor to the Pulpit*, 99-100.
† Jacob DeShazer, *Fuchida Remembered* , 19.

From time to time these two men teamed together in meetings throughout Japan, preaching the message of peace, forgiveness, and reconciliation. Fuchida once revisited Honolulu, Hawaii, scene of the Pearl Harbor attack, and handed out Bibles to people. He told one American, *"I came with bombs once, but now I come with the Bible. Jesus Christ is the answer."**

On 30 May 1976, Mitsuo Fuchida, warrior for Japan, turned warrior for God, went into the presence of the Savior he loved and served. Jake attended the funeral of his Japanese brother. The DeShazers have now retired from Japan and live in Salem, Oregon.

Both these men were once implacable, seemingly irreconcilable enemies. They were bound in cords of hatred and bitterness, willing to die in order to destroy each other.

Their conversions dramatically and completely changed their wills and hearts. They were transformed into seeking, forgiving peacemakers.

Everyone needs to reckon with certain questions about reconciliation: Is there someone in my life I need to forgive? Are there people I just can't tolerate? This world has more than its share of people living in an endless cycle of anger, slander, and malice. The bitter person remembers all the details of his real or imagined problem, and continually reviews those details. Loving and forgiving are not natural tendencies. They are supernatural. We cannot love and forgive in our own strength. Fuchida and DeShazer learned how to love from the Apostle Paul, who gave us this message of truth:

> *The love of Christ controls us, because we are convinced that one has died for all; therefore all have died [spiritually]. And he died for all, that those who live might live no longer for themselves but for him who for their sake died and was raised.* (2 Cor. 5:14–15)

---

† Jacob DeShazer, *Fuchida Remembered* , 19.

TWENTY-EIGHT

A BATTLEFIELD
AND A LILY

Okinawa: Where Prejudice Was Defeated

The real democratic American idea is, not that every man shall
be on level with every other man, but that every man shall have
liberty to be what God made him, without hindrance.
                                        —*Henry Ward Beecher*

We forget that "brainwashing" isn't always a bad word. Think
of its definition. Strictly speaking, to brainwash means to
cause a radical transformation of beliefs and mental attitude through
an intensive process of indoctrination. Such a process can be either good or bad.

Taking brainwashing in this broad sense, who was the best
brainwasher? An American admiral who was a highly decorated,
salty World War II hero, or Jesus Christ, the humble carpenter
from Galilee?

First, meet the admiral, a daring commander responsible for
America's first carrier task force during World War II. This task
force staged the first hit-and-run raids on the islands of Wake,
Marcus, and the Marshalls. He was a favorite of Navy and Marine
enlisted men because of his daring spirit, desire for victory, con-
tempt for the enemy, and vivid language.

Though a battle commander must exercise a certain disdain
for the enemy, how far should it go? Where is the delicate line
between disdain and hatred, between invigorating the morale of

the troops and subtly brainwashing (in the negative sense) for years to come?

One day when I was in the First Marine Division during World War II, we steamed into the harbor of Tulagi Island, near Guadalcanal in the Solomons, which had been won in a hard-fought battle. The US Armed Forces were using Tulagi as a rest-and-recreation area for the battle-weary men engaged in South Pacific island warfare.

As our ship, loaded with Marines, moved into the harbor, we saw a large billboard on shore. The men went to the shoreside of the ship to read it. It said something like this: "Kill Japs, kill Japs, and keep on killing Japs. The only good Jap is a dead Jap. Signed, Admiral ————." The men cheered.

The kind of scorn and prejudice that poured forth from the admiral in numerous press conferences and on that Tulagi billboard over forty years ago *still* affects certain Americans from that generation. I claim that this is a negative type of brainwashing.

Let me illustrate. An American businessman came into my office in the heart of downtown Tokyo some time ago. He was prosperous, well dressed, silver haired, and in his mid to late fifties. I introduced him to three of our Japanese staff. One of the questions he asked me, as we briefly conversed while standing in the middle of the office, was, "Do these Japs respond to the message of Christianity?"

When he said, "Japs," I winced and looked to see if any of the Japanese had heard him. If they had, it did not show on their placid faces as they continued their work. I thought it was just an oversight on the man's part and that it wouldn't slip out again.

We continued talking and, sure enough, he repeated the slur. This time I steered him to the door. Outside, I explained what the word "Jap" stood for and how it bought back harsh memories of the war. He was extremely embarrassed and apologetic and said he had meant no harm by these insensitive remarks.

He was, in a very real sense, a brainwashed man of his generation. Our entire national war effort had planted in his mind a subconscious prejudice that endured for over forty years.

Another time I was talking to a woman from this same age group at a conference in the United States. When she learned I was living in Japan, she said, "Somehow I just can't enjoy being around . . . " She couldn't finish her sentence, so I said, "Orientals?"

She answered, "Yes, uh-huh."

I said to her, "But Jesus was a Middle Easterner."

Prejudice has a strange inconsistency to it.

Radically Transformed Lives

Jesus Christ continues His work today on an international scale, brainwashing any man or woman who will voluntarily invite Him into his or her life. This is a positive brainwashing. He indoctrinates so intensively that a truly radical transformation takes place. He replaces prejudice with His own eternal value system. I'm writing this from Japan, where I've had the privilege of living amongst my former enemies for over thirty years.

The second brainwashed man I'll describe is Japanese. He was born as World War II ended, the offspring of a generation that Americans had been taught to hate and kill. This man is now in his early forties. His generation was caught between the traditions of old Japan (some of them good, some bad) and the new, postwar Japan.

As a high school student caught in the turmoil of these changes and with personal distresses in his own life, Toru Nagai began to investigate the life, death, and resurrection of the humble Galilean. Soon Nagai was hooked, and his mind was transformed. The "brainwashing" of the Nazarene began its steady progress in his thinking and character.

The dynamic influence of the Savior, which has continued over two thousand years, is based on love and forgiveness. It overcomes man's hatred of others because of race. He demonstrates true love. He continues to supernaturally implant it in the lives of His followers. This supernatural heart transplant to God's love replaces man's negative propaganda, such as "kill, kill, kill."

Nagai's belief and mental attitude changed steadily over the course of time. One time we were in Okinawa together on a work camp trip. There were twelve of us: nine Japanese and three Americans.

For more than a week we repainted several church exteriors and interiors and landscaped the grounds. Then we looked forward to some rest and sightseeing. This was the first time the Japanese with us had visited Okinawa, a beautiful coral island only seventy-five miles long and fifteen miles across at its widest.

In my life, Okinawa is more than just another subtropical island inhabited by a million people. It is a place where God touched my life in a special way on 17 June 1945, as the intense battle for possession of the island came to an end. It was there that a sniper's bullet pierced my throat and hand, subsequently altering my entire lifestyle.

Nagai and others on the work camp team requested a personal tour of the battlefield where I had been wounded. The place was a high, steep coral ridge called Kunishi Ridge by the Americans, running across the tip of the island, less than a mile from Itoman, Okinawa's largest fishing village on the southern coast.

I was somewhat apprehensive about what the reactions of my Japanese friends might be. As I told them the story of my injury, which took place about the time most of them were born, I realized it was their fathers' and uncles' generation against whom I had fought.

I told them how our tank, hit by antitank fire, was engulfed in flames and destroyed, how we were pinned down behind enemy lines. I pointed out the caves and ravines where the Japanese soldiers hid and unleashed sniper fire, seriously wounding three of us who had escaped from our tank.

After I had finished the story, and we stood there looking at the battlefield, Nagai quietly slipped away. He returned with a wild lily, bulb and all.

Nagai stepped forward and said to me, "Once our people were enemies with your people. But we want you to know that a change has come in our hearts because of the Prince of Peace. We who are standing here are a new generation. We want to dedicate our lives with you to the cause of sharing Jesus Christ with our people. Please accept this lily as a token of this dedication. Plant it back home in Tokyo in remembrance of this consecration."

We sealed that consecration with a prayer in that Okinawa sugar cane field. It was one of the most memorable moments in my life. Tears were flowing freely.

I planted the lily bulb in our garden in Tokyo. Each year as it bloomed, it reminded me of how well the humble Galilean had done His work in the life of Toru Nagai.

The Admiral had taught, "Kill!" The remnants of his teaching that remain in the minds of men and women are still painful, distant echoes of hatred and war.

Jesus Christ taught peace, faith, love, sacrifice, humility, and forgiveness. His teachings are positive, life-changing, and potent two thousand years after they were spoken. His message is intense and thorough. It still affects a radical transformation of beliefs and mental attitudes in the lives of people today—a transformation that works for good, not evil.

TWENTY-NINE

RECONCILIATION ON IWO JIMA
The Handshake of Peace

Forgiveness is better than revenge, for forgiveness is the sign of a gentle nature, but revenge is the sign of a savage nature.

—*Epictetus*

Iwo Jima—a volcanic speck in the vast western Pacific, immortalized during World War II by Japanese and American agony and valor. A haunting nightmare to thousands, a forgotten military relic to many, a magnetic fascination to former Marines, this mound of volcanic ash became in 1985 a symbol of reconciliation.

The battle of Iwo Jima began on February 19, 1945. It was the greatest toll of American casualties in the war, considering the length of the battle and the numbers involved. By sundown of the first evening, 566 US Marines and corpsmen lay dead or dying on the invasion beach. Robert Sherrod, combat correspondent, wrote, *"The first night on Iwo Jima can only be described as a nightmare in hell."*

On February 19, 1985, forty years to the day after that devastating battle, 170 Marine veterans, some with their wives, boarded four Air Force C-130 planes at Yokota Air Base in Japan to return to this infamous island of destruction. All wore on their group nametags, *Survivor of Iwo Jima*. About sixty of the one thousand Japanese soldiers who did not perish in the battle, along with seventy relatives and widows, were flown to Iwo by Japan's Self-Defense Force planes. It was a 660-mile trip to the scene of this World War II fight to the death. The objective of this traumatic return

233

was the dedication of both sides of a memorial stone of peace and reconciliation.

On 18 February 1985, although I had not fought on Iwo Jima, I felt a strong urging that God wanted me to go with these contingents. Prayer confirmed this feeling. What thoughts were going through the minds and hearts of these aging veterans, most in their sixties? In the words of a former Navy chaplain, John Pasanen, Iwo continued to represent *a past that has pervaded our dreams and haunted our sleepless nights.*

A Japanese woman who attended the ceremony said, "My brother was blown up at the base of Mount Suribachi, but I think today's ceremony would make him very content."

Many former Marines had vowed never to set foot on the volcanic ash sands of Iwo Jima again. But for those 170 who did return, the pathos and emotion, though almost overwhelming, was well worth it. Joe Buck of Cherokee, Oklahoma, summed up their feelings. Thinking back on the day of the landings, he said, "It was a sad day." But then observing the reunion and memorial service, he said, "I wouldn't have missed it for the world. I just wish some of my buddies could have lived to see it all."

For me the *handshake of peace* at the close of the dedication service was the highlight. There were tears, handshakes, and awkward hugs between former enemies as the process of reconciliation continued. Forgiveness and a new relationship was the atmosphere on both sides.

Marines made their way down to the landing beaches, and gathered in plastic sandwich bags some of the sand that once ran red to take home and share with those who didn't make the trip. The Japanese mood was summed up by Morimoto Katsuyoshi, a survivor and former Army surgeon, who is now very active in Japan's Iwo Jima Association: "It's not important who won or lost, but that both sides remember the place where our friends and relatives died."

A highlight, before we toured key points of interest on the island, was the unveiling of a memorial plaque of granite stone—an earthly attempt to memorialize the reconciliation between former enemies of forty years past. Our hearts were stirred at the message engraved in English on the seaward side where the Marines landed and in Japanese on the landward side where the Japanese defended:

REUNION OF HONOR

ON THE 40TH ANNIVERSARY OF THE BATTLE
OF IWO JIMA,
AMERICAN & JAPANESE VETERANS MET AGAIN
ON THESE SAME SANDS,
THIS TIME IN PEACE AND FRIENDSHIP.
WE COMMEMORATE OUR COMRADES,
LIVING AND DEAD, WHO FOUGHT HERE
WITH BRAVERY & HONOR,
AND WE PRAY TOGETHER THAT OUR SACRIFICES
ON IWO JIMA
WILL ALWAYS BE REMEMBERED AND NEVER BE REPEATED.
FEBRUARY 19, 1985.
3RD, 4TH, 5TH DIVISION ASSOCIATIONS:
USMC; AND THE ASSOCIATION OF IWO JIMA.

That same evening, as I crammed into the jump seat of the C-130 transport returning to Japan, I knew I had witnessed one of man's finest dramas of reconciliation. Implacable enemies in a struggle to the death four decades ago, with few exceptions, were now healed of past resentments and bitterness. It had taken much effort, toil, sweat, planning, and time on both sides to bring this to pass.

Reflection on this caused me to think of the passage in the New Testament that speaks of reconciliation between God and man through the Christ, who is the Great Reconciler:

Now in Christ Jesus you who once were far away have been bought near through the blood of Christ. For He Himself is our peace, who has made the two one and has destroyed the barrier, the dividing wall of hostility . . . His purpose was to create in Himself one new man out of the two, thus making peace, and in this one body to reconcile both of them to God through the cross, by which he put to death their hostility. (Eph. 2:13–16)

We have created a barrier, erecting a wall of hostility toward God by our rebellion, implacability, and failure to accept His forgiveness. Forty years seems like a long time to bring about reconciliation between two antagonists. Yet for many of us, God has patiently waited throughout our earthly lifetimes to forgive us, embrace us, and give us the handclasp of eternal peace through His Son. All we need to do is reach out in childlike faith to the Great Reconciler.

THE JERK
Judging Others

You can't clear your own fields while you're counting the rocks on your neighbor's farm.

—*Joan Welsh*

I met him while my wife and I were on one of the most historical and emotional trips of our well-traveled lives. We were back in Okinawa in June 1995 for the fiftieth commemoration of the last battle of World War II.

Remembering that solemn occasion were a handful of Japanese military veteran survivors, Okinawan civilians who had lost untold thousands of relatives and countrymen, and approximately 700 US veterans. Altogether, these three groups lost over 230,000 killed in that approximate three-month holocaust on an island seventy-five miles long by three-to-fifteen miles wide.

At Peace Memorial Park on the southern tip of Okinawa, the names of all the nearly one-quarter-million dead Okinawan, Japanese and Americans, are etched into granite slab walls that make the Vietnam Wall look like a miniature. The beautiful memorial park overlooks the Pacific Ocean and China Sea. Far below the well-kept lawn at the top of the cliff are the rugged coral rocks upon which many Okinawans threw their frail, starving bodies rather than surrender to US Forces. Japanese wartime propaganda urged suicide rather than fall into the hands of the "rapacious, murderous Americans."

The Jerk? I want to tell you about him. He came into my life so unexpectedly and was a kind of spoiler to all the emotions and memories that kept churning through my heart nonstop on this historical, coral, semitropical island. But first it is important for you to know how traumatic this trip was for me.

We had returned to Okinawa several days before the large body of veterans in our particular tour arrived. We met some American friends who live there and others stationed on bases. Also Okinawan friends, some of whom became Christians through our ministry when we lived on Okinawa from 1952 to 1956. The two oldest of our five children, Holly and Laurel, were born there in Quonset huts that served as a hospital.

On the exact day and approximate hour of the morning fifty years previously (17 June 1945), about thirty of us held a memorial service within a few meters of where several of us had been gravely wounded in the battle. Jerry Atkinson, K. C. Smith, and I were gunned down by a Japanese sniper behind enemy lines. Jerry and I were left for dead. The three of us had survived the destruction of our tank by Japanese antitank fire. God miraculously delivered all three of us from the hands of a desperate enemy.

Three of our married children had come to Okinawa to be with us for three of the ten days we were on the island: Paul, John, and Heidi. What a great personal privilege to have them join us in that fiftieth memorial service. Soon after our children left Okinawa, my wife and I joined our veteran's tour group. It didn't seem to take very long to have our first encounter with The Jerk. There is a tremendous camaraderie among Marines even meeting one another for the first time.

However, every once in a while you run into a Marine who rubs you the wrong way and you wonder how he ever became one. That's the way I felt about this guy. Somehow in the ten tour buses that our group of several hundred toured the island in, we invariably ended up on the same bus with—what else can I call him but a jerk!

To be around Marine veterans for extended periods means you inevitably hear foul language. But this guy, I'll call him "Larry" for this story, outdid all Marines with his gutter words.

Okinawa in June was hot and humid—in the 90s—and though the buses were air conditioned, we were off these vehicles as much or more than on them. It didn't take long to be drenched in sweat, especially when climbing ridges and hills trying to identify old battlefields where death and destruction were our twin companions fifty years previously.

Feelings and emotions ran deep for buddies lost and units decimated in such places as Kakazu Ridge, Hill 60, Wilson's Ridge, Wana Draw and Ridge, Dakeshi Ridge, Shuri Castle, and many others.

The sweat didn't matter, but when you got back on the bus a cool drink of water was mighty fine. I noticed one day that Larry, sitting across from me, gave out the warm bottles of water to others and kept the cold one for himself. But that isn't all!

One time after an extensive walking tour of Shuri Castle, now completely restored, headquarters and underground command center for General Ushijima's Thirty-Second Imperial Army, my wife and I reboarded our bus and headed for our seats. Larry had spread himself and his belongings out over both of our seats.

"Excuse me, but those are the seats we were occupying," I said in typical, polite Marine fashion.

Larry replied flippantly, "Oh, there's plenty of room back there," pointing toward the back.

Not wanting to hassle, we found two seats together in the rear. Sure enough, shortly the couple that had originally been siting there came to claim their places. It was musical bus seats. I went back up and tried to patiently explain to Larry—again in typical, humble Marine manner—and asked him to move to his original single seat. Reluctantly and grumpily and with deliberate slow, resentful movements, he returned to his own place.

I thought, *I'm glad we got that settled with a minimum of hassle— and I'm glad I won't have anymore dealings with that guy! We have only one more full day of touring the island.*

That last full day on Okinawa was extremely important to about two dozen of us. One bus, at our request, was going all the way down to the southern part, especially to Kunishi Ridge where all of us had fought steadily for seven days before it was finally captured. The already badly depleted First Marine Division had suffered 1,150 casualties in our sector of the Ridge alone.'

The next morning, wanting a good seat on the front of Bus #6, I boarded early. My wife chose not to come. So far there were only two or three other Marines aboard. Great! I was filled with eager expectations of what the day would hold, especially at historical Kunishi Ridge. From where I sat I could see other passengers approaching.

Here came Larry. I prepared to give him a civil "good morning" as he boarded and headed toward the rear in the almost empty bus. He acknowledged my greeting and then paused in the aisle. Guess what?

"Can I sit here with you?"

What could I say? "Yeah, sure," I replied with a half-smile. But in my heart I was groaning and saying, *Oh, no, not all day long riding around half of Okinawa with this guy*. At the same time though, I knew deep down inside that it was really God who had made this arrangement. He wanted to teach me some lessons. I knew, too, that very possibly this was Larry's way of apologizing for the events of yesterday. Maybe he had no friends. It seemed that he needed one.

During that long, hot, humid day Larry and I became buddies. We shared our stories of events that took place in our lives during the deadly, no-quarter battle of Okinawa. We both acknowledged that because of the grace of God we were survivors. Kunishi Ridge and other battlefields had eagerly reached out to snatch and destroy our lives, but we were spared for then unknown purposes.

The climax of our Return to Okinawa Tour on the final half-day was a Memorial breakfast. After the meal and several speakers it was my privilege to give the final invocation prayer.

Afterwards, Larry sought me out in the huge hotel dining room. With tears in his eyes, he eagerly grasped my hand, "Bob, that was just one helluva prayer. Thank you. I hope we meet again!" He felt that he had found a real friend.

Larry didn't really know how I had misjudged him—how uncompassionate and cold my heart had been toward him. I had wrongly looked on the outward appearance and had not seen beyond the crude words and actions of my newfound buddy. I was a very poor example of my compassionate Savior.

My wife and I went up to our room to finish packing. As I took a final look around the room I stopped in front of the mirror—and came face to face with the real Jerk.

VII. REUNIONS: THE
SEMPER FIDELIS SPIRIT

Don Thompson, D.I. Bahde, Bill Henahan, Jerry Atkinson, Bob Boardman,
MuMu Moore,   Pappy Gore.

THIRTY-ONE

MULTIPLYING FAITH ON IWO JIMA

A Son Remembers His Father

Faith is deliberate confidence in the character of God whose ways you may not understand at the time.

—*Oswald Chambers*

It is personally a great privilege and special calling to serve as chaplain of the Marine Corps Tanker's Association and also chaplain of the Evergreen State of Washington Chapter of the First Marine Division Association. I enjoy writing a regular column for the Tanker's Association magazine, although it is never an easy task. Some of the responses both to the "Chaplain's Corner" and to some of the pamphlets I've published have made the toil and time well worth it.

Here are two responses from former Marines:

Your recollections in the pamphlet *Unforgettable Men in Unforgettable Times* evoked many memories and emotions for me. My father, Curtis Jorstad (deceased 27 August 1991), served with the Twenty-Seventh Marine Regiment on Iwo Jima as an infantryman—a scout-observer for the heavy gun platoon commanded by Gunnery Sgt. John Basilone (Medal of Honor recipient on Guadalcanal). Dad made it through to the end of the battle, which was something of a miracle. The 27th was reclassified to a composite battalion towards the end of the fight, able to muster only 500 Marines out of an initial 3,000, plus replacements. My service with our beloved Marine Corps took place in the early 1970s with A Company, First Tank Battalion. I had the honor and privilege of duty with a few of the last World War II Marine veterans on active duty. Our country has never produced a better generation of patriots, nor our Corps a better group of Marines, before or since.

After World War II, Curtis Jorstad, Tim's father, became a pastor, devoting his life with *Semper Fidelis* faithfulness and intensity to helping others. Tim sent me a copy of his own eulogy read at the funeral service of his father:

In contemplating our father's life, I continually return to certain words, three in particular . . . devotion, sacrifice, people. Dad had learned many of his virtues from his family growing up in Minnesota. The Lutheran church was another strong foundation. Many of Dad's qualities, such as strength, modesty, sincerity, and humor, reflect his childhood and rearing. I believe the cauldron of Iwo Jima finally cast my father's overall character as a man. Twenty-two-year-old Curtis fought, start to finish, in a thirty-six-day battle for eight square miles, which cost 26,000 lives. In the midst of the horror, Dad saw beyond the carnage at hand and understood meaning and merit in the sacrifice and devotion so incredibly displayed. Many say the measure of a life is if it made a positive difference or not. My father made a positive difference on a legion of people. Personally, Curtis ennobled my life. I am humbled to be his son. Please join me in picking up my dad's guidon. Let us all take increased devotion to one another and the faiths we hold so dear.

The challenge to live a life of faith and devotion can't be expressed much more effectively than from this father and son. He being dead yet speaks!

Just a few months before a planned trip to Atlanta, I received a letter from Jim Haygood of Woodstock, Georgia. He joined the Marine Corps in 1946 at the age of seventeen and served in the Second Tank Battalion. I had never met Jim, but he thanked me for one of the "Chaplain's Corner" features I'd written. He also invited me to visit him and his wife if I was ever in the Atlanta area.

When I did go to Atlanta, I was able to meet Jim and his wife for lunch. As two former Marines, we had a great time comparing notes. Just three weeks after this luncheon, I received word that Jim died suddenly in his home of a massive heart attack. He was sixty-three. Job said, *"Only a few years will pass before I go on the journey of no return."*

I telephoned Jim's wife, Betty, to try to console her over Jim's passing. She said that Jim had a personal relationship with Jesus Christ and was ready for that unexpected and traumatic moment when he took the journey of no return. But whereas I thought I would encourage Betty, her faith challenged me. She said, "I find no fault in my Lord over Jim's unexpected death."

Tim, Curtis, Jim, and Betty . . . multiplying faith that speaks to us by death and by life. The Savior sums up this truth: *"Truly, truly, I say to you, unless a grain of wheat falls into the earth and dies, it remains alone; but if it dies, it bears much fruit"* (John 12:24).

THIRTY-TWO

THE FOUNTAIN
OF YOUTH

Attitude Determines Age

Youth is not properly definable by age. It is a spirit of daring, creating, asserting life, and openly relating to the world.

—*Malcolm Boyd*

I remember my youth and the feeling that will never come back any more—the feeling that I could last forever, outlast the sea, the earth, and all men.

—*Joseph Conrad*

A Marine reunion of any kind can be a spiritual catharsis as the exciting, adventurous days of our youth come back into focus with men who became comrades for life. Sea stories abound and are sometimes embellished. Dim, fading memories are jogged and the names of buddies are remembered. The grog flows and the past glows.

Every cluster of warriors seems to have an individual or two who can recount events and people that amaze the rest of us. Who can match Bill Henahan, MuMu Moore, Phil Morell, and Benedict Wolfe as storytellers? Storyteller First Class should be their rate.

As I've pondered this phenomenon of excitement and closeness, the words of Shakespeare may explain it best: "*We few, we happy few, we band of brothers, for he who shed his blood with me, shall be my brother*" (Henry V).

247

These are men who have shed their very life's blood—or were willing to do that at great risk. There is no higher price to pay than the shedding of blood. Can I ever forget Bud Brenkert and Old Man Christensen being willing to lay down their lives for me? And Jerry Atkinson's daring and successful attempt to save the life of an unknown Marine badly wounded and exposed to heavy artillery fire on Okinawa's Machinato Airfield? These and others are truly a band of incredible brothers.

Why are there so many older salts at most reunions in comparison to younger veterans? Perhaps because young men think more about the future than the past. Conversely, as we grow older we tend to focus more on the exciting past and seek to recapture fading memories. Growing older we may have a sense of historical perspective to see what God allowed us to live through in days gone by.

Is all of this part of a search for the proverbial *Fountain of Youth?* Perhaps. It is important to remember the *past*, to live in the *present* and hope and prepare for the *future*. We need to guard against becoming dusty relics in a Marine museum.

> We may retire from a vocation, but never from life. God wants us to be players not spectators, even though we may not be first string anymore. Nobody automatically stays young in heart and mind. Living old is a choice we make; it is not an inevitable sentence from Mother Nature and Father Time. No matter how old you are, count for something, even if it's only that you listen to the younger crowd, pray for them, and encourage them to live for God.
>
> —*Warren Wiersbe*

Years ago I read the following about staying young in heart and not growing cynical and pessimistic. Every so often I challenge myself by rereading it:

> Youth is not a time of life—it is a state of mind; it is a temper of the will, a quality of the imagination, a vigor of the emotions, a predominance of courage over timidity, of the appetite for adventure over love of ease.

Nobody grows old by merely living a number of years; people grow old only by deserting their ideals. Years wrinkle the skin, but to give up enthusiasm wrinkles the soul. Worry, doubt, self-distrust, fear and despair—these are the long, long years that bow the head and turn the growing spirit back to dust.

You are as young as your faith, as old as your doubt; as young as your self-confidence, as old as your fear, as young as your hope, as old as your despair.

So long as your heart receives messages of beauty, cheer, courage, grandeur, and power from the earth, from man and from the Infinite, so long as you are young.

When the wires are all down and the central place of your heart is covered with the snow of pessimism and the ice of cynicism, then you are grown old indeed and God have mercy on your soul.

The Bible makes clear that the Fountain of Youth is not physical, but is in our mind, in our attitude and the key is spiritual. The Lord Jesus Christ unlocks the secret and invites us to drink at the Fountain of Life when he said: *"If anyone thirst, let him come to Me and drink. He who believes in Me, as the Scripture has said, 'Out of his heart shall flow rivers of living water"* (John 7:37–38).

Finally, for those of us and our thinning ranks who are march-stepping toward the journey of no return, here is a prayer of wisdom from the incomparable Psalmist:

Now also when I am old and gray headed,
O God, do not forsake me,
Until I declare Your strength to this generation,
Your power to everyone who is to come." (Psalm 71:18)

THIRTY-THREE

OF HEROES
AND CELEBRITIES
A Doggie Hero

A hero is a central figure in any important event or period, admired and honored for courage, outstanding nobility of character, exploits and achievements—and regarded as an ideal or model.
—*Webster's Dictionary*

Medal of Honor recipients are certainly true wartime heroes. In World War II eighty-one Marines were awarded the MOH (the highest medal awarded for bravery in combat), forty-eight of them posthumously; in the Korean War there were forty-two recipients; and fifty-seven Marines received the MOH in Vietnam. The exploits and sacrifices of these 180 men fit many of the above dictionary qualifications for becoming a true hero.

A hero is basically someone who we want to emulate. The Communist world creates heroes and gives them to the people to follow and imitate. They are foisted upon the masses by omnipresent statues and busts, many of immense size. There are ubiquitous posters, photographs, prizes, books, and publications.

But in our Western world, we are equally guilty by allowing our materialistic decadence to foist upon us, not heroes, but celebrities to idolize. Clever salesmanship has created a monster out of certain skills and talent in the fields of music, sports, business, film, media, and politics—yes, and in religion, too. And it keeps growing to grotesque proportions.

There are still heroes in today's world, but they are being over-shadowed by celebrities. Daniel Boorstin, historian and Pulitzer Prize-winning author says:

> The hero is known for achievements, the celebrity for well knownness. The hero reveals the possibilities of human nature, the celebrity reveals the possibilities of the press and the media. Celebrities are people who make the news, but heroes are people who make history. Time makes heroes but dissolves celebrities.

Heroes can become celebrities. Often they do not seek that status. How they handle that adulation is critical to their reputation. In June 1995 on the Return to Okinawa for the fiftieth commemoration of that last battle of World War II, several of us Marine veterans came upon an Army veteran named Desmond Doss as we all examined a very tough ridge the Army had taken at great cost. Doss had the Medal of Honor around his neck.

Doss, from Lynchburg, Virginia, was a conscientious objector, but was drafted as a medic. Though severely wounded himself and at great personal cost, he lowered other wounded over the cliff to safety. He said to us, "I never thought I deserved this medal. I was just doing what I was trained to do." Doss was a true humble hero in our books.

Here is Desmond Doss's official Medal of Honor citation as a PFC in the Medical Detachment, 307th Infantry, 77th Infantry Division:

> Citation: He was a company aid man when the First Battalion assaulted a rugged escarpment 400 feet high. As our troops gained the summit, a heavy concentration of artillery, mortar and machine gun fire crashed into them, inflicting approximately 75 casualties and driving the others back. PFC Doss refused to seek cover and remained in the fire-swept area with the many stricken, carrying them one by one to the edge of the escarpment and there lowering

them on a rope-supported litter down the face of a cliff to friendly hands.

On 2 May, he exposed himself to heavy rifle and mortar fire in rescuing a wounded man 200 yards forward of the lines on the same escarpment; and two days later he treated four men who had been cut down while assaulting a strongly defended cave, advancing through a shower of grenades to within eight yards of enemy forces in a cave's mouth, where he dressed his comrades' wounds before making four separate trips under fire to evacuate them to safety.

On 5 May, he unhesitatingly braved enemy shelling and small-arms fire to assist an artillery officer. He applied bandages, moved his patient to a spot that afforded protection from small-arms fire and, while artillery and mortar shells fell close by, painstakingly administered plasma. Later that day, when an American was severely wounded by fire from a cave, PFC Doss crawled to him where he had fallen 25 feet from the enemy position, rendered aid, and carried him 100 yards to safety while continually exposed to enemy fire.

On 21 May, in a night attack on high ground near Shuri, he remained in exposed territory while the rest of his company took cover, fearlessly risking the chance that he would be mistaken for an infiltrating Japanese and giving aid to the injured until he was himself seriously wounded in the legs by the explosion of a grenade. Rather than call another aid man from cover, he cared for his own injuries and waited five hours before litter bearers reached him and started carrying him to cover. The trio was caught in an enemy tank attack and PFC Doss, seeing a more critically wounded man nearby, crawled off the litter and directed the bearers to give their first attention to the other man. Awaiting the litter bearers' return, he was again struck, this time suffering a compound fracture of one arm. With magnificent fortitude he bound a rifle stock to his shattered arm as a splint and then crawled 300 yards over rough terrain to the aid station. Through his outstanding bravery and unflinching determination in the face of desperately dangerous conditions PFC Doss saved the lives of many soldiers. His name became a symbol throughout the Seventy-Seventh Infantry Division for outstanding gallantry far above and beyond the call of duty.

Col. Mitch Paige, USMC, Retired, is now the only surviving MOH recipient of the ground war on Guadalcanal. His attitude about having the medal is similar to Doss's and is described in Chapter 6 of this book.

In trying to think through on the ingredients that make a hero, it involves most always overcoming adversity, suffering, and making a sacrifice. It often means facing hostile adversaries and never giving up on moral and religious convictions.

Yet there is another kind of hero. *"The man or woman who rules their own spirit is greater than the one who takes a city"* (Prov. 16:32). H. W. Beecher said, "The world's battlefields have been in the heart chiefly; more heroism has been displayed in the household, than on the most memorable battlefields of history."

Someone has well said, *"Tell me who you admire and I'll tell you who you are."* It is a good exercise to list our heroes. Then we will gain insights into who we are.

All earthly heroes have feet of clay. I know of only one person who measures up to all the criteria for being a complete, true hero: Jesus Christ. He alone can give the courage we need to rule our spirits, to overcome the waywardness of our hearts. He can give the humility to be an unsung, unrecognized "hero" in the midst of materialistic celebrityism.

"The crowds were astonished at His teaching" (Matt. 7:28).
"The Son of Man has authority to forgive sins" (Mark 2:10).

THIRTY-FOUR

ABANDON TANKS!

Old Tankers Never Die, They Just Lose Track

The last three tanks I had the privilege of driving, I had to abandon. These do not count a tank I was driving on Peleliu that was severely disabled by a visually set off Japanese land mine that must have been a rigged 500-pound aerial bomb. The Japanese detonation man on Bloody Nose Ridge pushed the plunger ever so slightly prematurely.

The tremendous explosion of the bomb in front of our tank and under our protruding 75mm gun drove shrapnel into the tube of the gun, indenting the inside of the barrel destroying the gun. The crater in front of the tank was so huge that if we had driven our Sherman into it we couldn't have gotten out.

If the explosion had been directly under the tank as it was supposed to be, there is no doubt our thirty-three ton machine would have been flipped over. A good buddy, Nick Backovich, was the assistant driver and bow gunner. The entire five-man crew was greatly shaken, but by God's grace, there were no casualties. But back to the last three abandoned tanks.

1. In the battle of Okinawa in mid-June 1945, while serving with C Company, First Tank Battalion—Lt. Walter MuMu Moore, Executive Officer—something happened to our tank as we moved against strong Japanese resistance on Kunishi Ridge. We were either hit and disabled or broke a track in No Man's Valley. We all escaped safely.

Later that day in No Man's Valley, I returned to our disabled tank riding inside another tank with a combat engineer. We planned to booby trap our abandoned tank so the Japanese wouldn't blow it up in the night. I jumped over onto our tank. I also needed to disable the .30-caliber, sky-mount machine gun. As I turned the driving rod one quarter turn with a screwdriver to remove the back plate, a Japanese sniper, aiming for me, hit the machine gun, splattering tiny fragments of hot metal into my hand. No Purple Heart for that one.

2. One or two days later, on Father's Day, 17 June 1945, while driving tank for Lt. Jerry "Ack Ack" Atkinson, just past Kunishi Ridge, two of our few remaining tanks in C Company were knocked out by Japanese 76mm antitank guns. In Bud Brenkert's and "Old Man" Christensen's tank, "Scuddley" Hoffman was killed, as was Robert Bennett in ours.

   In Chapter 1, "Unforgettable Men in Unforgettable Times," and in Chapter 24, "The Father's Day Massacre" by Colonel Moore, the story of our ensuing escape from behind enemy lines is told. God's strong right arm in delivering several of us, though severely wounded, from what seemed like certain death, was undeniable.

   It may seem strange to some, but probably not to most tankers, that abandoning a tank that has taken us through so much was like losing an old and familiar friend. They seem to develop their own personalities!

3. North Bend, Oregon 26 August 1995. Fifty years after Okinawa, at our national Marine Corps Tanker's Association reunion, was my chance to again drive a tank! Surely I would not have to abandon this steel vehicle, a smooth running, powerful M-47. Blackie Verdugo had won the top prize in a raffle—to drive Mr. Shirley Laird's reconditioned tank at the reunion. Because of back and leg problems, Blackie could not operate the foot pedals in the tank and graciously offered me his place, which I eagerly and gratefully accepted.

Laird gave me instructions and rode on top of the tank to make sure all went well. Off we went. What a thrill after fifty years! I drove about one quarter of a mile on the course at Pacific Coast Recreation, when suddenly there was some loud, repeated backfiring and we slowly jerked to a stop, the engine dead. Out of gas!

Abandon tank!

Keenly disappointed, we were soon picked up by one of Laird's trucks and taken back to the car park.

Slowly, over a fifty-year period, I'm beginning to get the message. I should have been in Marine infantry! Semper Fi.

THIRTY-FIVE

EPITAPHS

A Summary of Your LIfe

To one swell guy
Our buddy, a great guy, & a fine Marine
A big guy with a bigger heart

These were some of the simple inscriptions on the 621 crude, makeshift graves in the First Marine Division cemetery on Guadalcanal in 1942. They were spelled out with palm fronds and sticks by their buddies who survived.

Is it morbid to think or talk about this subject? I don't believe so, since death along with taxes are the two inescapable things in this life. In a one-year period since we last met, the 14,000 member First Marine Division Association, fifty-four years after Guadalcanal, has recorded 280 deaths that are known for sure.

At all Returned Soldiers League Clubs scattered throughout Australia, *every day* at 6:00 p.m., they lower the lights and everyone repeats a litany that ends with the words, *"Lest we forget."* They honor their fallen comrades. It is important to do that and also to think seriously about our own imminent departure.

Through the years in the course of our many travels, I have visited military and civilian cemeteries around the world: Europe, Japan, Korea, New Guinea, Australia, New Zealand, Russia, and Hawaii. Perhaps there is no more solemn scene than to view the precise rows of crosses, punctuated here and there by a Star of David, in our military cemeteries at home and abroad.

One of the most poignant epitaphs I have ever read was on the headstone of a sixteen-year-old US soldier in France: *God will tell us why some day, He came and took you away.*

Some Marines, Navy personnel, and soldiers who have finished a battle and remain in the area, have the opportunity to visit the cemetery of deceased comrades and be involved in the memorial service. Other combatants, like myself, never had that opportunity because of being moved from the battlefield as units at the conclusion of combat or because of being a casualty.

In downtown Seattle, the city has honored the names of their war dead in a prominent plaza. The names of each one are inscribed into stone slabs and in the center is this moving epitaph:

> Forever engraved upon the hearts of a grateful people are these names of our brave sons and daughters who made the supreme sacrifice their final payment on the price of our freedom.

One day I stood in the plaza reading this beautiful and fitting inscription and some of the names of our heroic war dead through many years. I couldn't help notice the contrast of peace in the plaza with the hustle and bustle of the downtown passersby. It seemed that so few pause to think about the price paid for our freedom—and to think upon their own eternal destiny.

In the little Australian town of Shepparton, New South Wales, I visited the cemetery in 1987. On the gravestone of John Welch, who died in 1879 at age fifty-six, was this unforgettable inscription:

> Remember me as you pass by,
> As you are now, so once was I,
> As I am now, so you will be,
> Prepare yourself to follow me.

John Welch challenges us to prepare ourselves to follow him. If you could write your own epitaph, how would it read? What would the summary of your life be?

The Bible has some very insightful and powerful summaries of the lives of men and women which could well be their epitaphs:

> REHOBOAM: *"He did evil, because he did not prepare his heart to seek the Lord."*
> UZZIAH: *"He sought God; God prospered him, he became strong, but then his heart was lifted up with pride."*
> ABEL: *"He died, but through his faith [in Christ] he is still speaking."*

Psalm 90 tells us to think carefully and deeply about our present lives and pending deaths. Let us not be like some of the thoughtless passersbys in downtown Seattle who can't seem to focus on their brave countrymen's sacrifices. Our allotted years pass so quickly—as a story that is told and soon forgotten. Therefore, the psalmist prays, as we also ought to: *"Teach us to number our days, that we may apply our hearts to wisdom"* (Psalm 90:12).

Tomorrow's epitaph should cause you and me to think carefully and deeply about today's actions, thoughts and words. Jesus Christ, God's priceless gift to us, died for our sins and rose again from the grave to give us hope. He was the glorious presence of God upon earth. If we know and love Him and walk with Him daily, He will grant us this epitaph by His grace:

> *Well done, good and faithful servant, enter into the presence of your Lord.*

EPILOGUE

At this stage of my life I have been allowed to live four years past the biblical "three score and ten." That's seventy-four, for those with computers! Jean is right at seventy. We feel, even with all of life's hardships and trials, blessed beyond our ability to express it. To date our health and strength are reasonable.

Our generation is pounding down the homestretch of life, toward the finish line. We never lose sight of the fact that so many of our peers, including Jean's oldest brother lost in the Philippines during World War II, finished the race in the prime of their youth on some Pacific island or shore—or on the continents of Europe or North Africa.

World War II purchased a great heritage through the blood and sacrifice of so many—not just for our beloved country but for the world. May these stories not only remind us of that alarming price but add to our appreciation of the men and women who gladly—and often fearfully—stood in the gap in time of national and worldwide crisis.

Adoniram Judson, who labored in Burma in the nineteenth century, once said, *"I am not talented, but I can plod."* I personally don't think he knew himself that well, for he translated the Bible and portions of it into over thirty languages and dialects!

Most good things that have happened in my life have come through steady perseverance, toil, and God's blessing—not talent. I have some occasions to speak publicly here and there but never in a thundering manner. And no one can ever accuse me of shouting at my wife and children.

More and more I realize the importance and power of the pen—the printed page—in order to bring something into being that didn't previously exist, something that would touch lives, young and old alike. In *Unforgettable Men in Unforgettable Times* I have tried to write by looking into my own soul and also from experience, rather than just about some "subject."

I hope and pray that young and old Marines, as well as veterans from all branches of the armed forces, will receive challenges, ideas, and enlightenment for the onward path. Also that young people and families will be strengthened and, as General Krulak said, *"Look for the light."*

Jean and I are deeply impressed by the quality of officers and NCOs that lead the Marine Corps today. The ones that I have had the privilege of meeting and knowing are some of our nation's finest leaders. Many are God-fearing men. May their number multiply.

All of the men from C Company listed on the dedication page are still in touch with one another, even though most only by correspondence. This is one of the great privileges of life for Jean and me. Over fifty years have passed, showing that these are truly unforgettable men.

These are extremely critical days for our nation and its God-given heritage. Spiritual darkness and moral degradation seem to be closing in, causing the love of many to turn cold. As Capt. Julian Dusenbury raised the flag over Shuri Castle and as the five Marines and a corpsman raised the Stars and Stripes on Mount Suribachi, so may we raise the banner of our great God and the principles of right and justice unashamedly for all to see. Semper Fidelis!

ACKNOWLEDGMENTS

Writing a book is the nearest a man gets to having a baby.
                                                    —*John R. Stott*

A writer needs encouragement along the way on his pilgrimage, in his travail, more than most people realize. The following people have done that in small and great ways. Add all of that support together and the finished composition brings satisfaction to the soul and, hopefully, beneficence to many readers.

- Gen. Charles Krulak, USMC, for his step of faith in the writing of the foreword. I am deeply humbled, honored, and thankful.
- Lt. Gen. Frank Libutti, USMC, for his encouragement of my writing endeavors when he commanded the First Marine Division not too long ago.
- Col. Jerry Brown (Ret.), USMC, likewise through the last several years has been a true friend and great support.
- Ruth Bell Graham has been a dear friend to Jean and me for many years. There is no doubt in our minds that she is a key to Billy's life and spiritual power.
- Monte "Chuck" Unger, my editor, who encouraged and counseled me in my beginnings as a writer many years ago. Working with him on this challenging venture has again, as with my first book, kept me on the right course. He is a committed colleague to Marine ideals, even though he was a Doggie, and is a coach, cheerleader, and critic.

- Brock Brockinton. Brock was a company commander on Okinawa of I and K Companies, Third Battalion, Fifth Regiment. This stately Southern gentleman has been a joy to know and is a great inspiration.
- Chuck Dean, Garlen and Anita Jackson, and their staff at Selah Publishing. Chuck is a former 173rd Army Airborne in Vietnam who experienced a lot of combat. They have been most helpful, supportive, and understanding of my purpose.

The Artists

- John Flack. I'm grateful to John, veteran of Okinawa and North China, for the front cover concept.
- Don Enright, World War II US Navy B-24 nose gunner, veteran of many air patrols in the Pacific, and long-time friend, is a renowned artist who painted the front cover in watercolor.
- Ren Narita, third generation Japanese American and close friend, did the line drawings. His and Dorothy's six children are priceless.

Marine Mates and Buddies (I can name only a few)

- Col. Walter "MuMu" Moore (Ret.), USMC, gathered the interviews and put together Chapter 24, for which I am indebted. I have wanted to write a monograph on the life of this colorful, intelligent, gung ho Christian character, but for private reasons he has turned this down.
- Old buddies Joe Alvarez, Jerry "The Sieve" Atkinson, D. I. Bahde, Nick Backovich, Bud Brenkert, "Old Man" Christensen, and "Wild Bill" Henahan have given invaluable material for Chapters 21 and 24 . . . and to my life and the privilege of knowing them.
- Other Marines throughout the book who have allowed me to write their stories and relate their experiences are truly unforgettable men! Thank you. When you, the reader, read these various accounts, stop to give a word of gratitude to God for these defenders of our nation.

Special Encouragers

- Don Simpson, editor of my first book, and Leon Alderman, Commander (Ret.), US Navy, have always and consistently urged me on.
- Lt. Col. Dave Becker, USMC, and his wife, Pam, have had a special part in our lives in relation to this book.
- Don Gagnon, editor of *The Tanker's Newsletter*, and Jim Collier, past president of the Marine Corps Tankers Association, have our greatest gratitude for their consistent support.
- Boyce Clark, a veteran of Korea, past president of the Evergreen Chapter of the First Marine Division Association, and his wife, Charlotte. Boyce is a quiet, dynamic Marine recruiter and doer of excellent works.
- Mitch Paige, MOH, Chapter 7, continues his struggle to regain physical health. He fights this battle today with the same courage he displayed on Guadalcanal, with the support of his dear wife, Marilyn.
- Ron York, Korea veteran, Marine buddy, and Navigator colaborer. He and his wife, Joyce, always challenge and stimulate our spirits.
- Mitsuo Sasaki, Tokyo attorney, and his creative wife, Yumiko. They believe in the power of the written word and energetically promulgate it near and far.
- Marines at large and friends who have graciously backed the construction and publishing of *Unforgettable Men*. It would have been difficult to do the book without them. Jean and I cannot express adequate thanksgiving.
- Last, but not least, my beloved wife of forty-five years, Jean, who has done lots of helpful proofreading. And my five children: Holly, Laurel, Paul, John, and Heidi—all married. Heidi also did an outstanding job of proofreading. Their wholehearted backing enabled, encouraged, and strengthened me in this travail. This is also for our six grandchildren and great granddaughter.

To order additional copies of

UNFORGETTABLE MEN
IN
UNFORGETTABLE TIMES

signed by the author (please indicate clearly to
whom you would like it signed), send

$12.99 (softcover)
or
$19.99 (hardcover)

plus $3.95 shipping and handling (add $1.00 S&H for each additional book). Please make check or money order (please do not
send cash) to:

Bob Boardman
P. O. Box 25001
Seattle, WA 98165–1901

Also order by Email (include mailing address) to:
rrboardman@aol.com

for credit card orders please call:
(800) 917-2665

By the Author Robert Boardman

A Higher Honor

- Foreword by Senator Mark Hatfield

Intriguing observations of Japanese honor and commitment in peacetime and in war. Wounded in a war of hate, Robert Boardman, returned to Japan, land of his former enemy to live and minister for 33 years, in order to wage a different war with different weapons.

Choice vignettes about the honor and commitment of the Japanese and two nations, America and Japan – who progressed from war to a time of reconciliation and peace.

Penetrating insights into the Japanese culture and customs.

To order
A Higher Honor

send $8.00 plus $2.95 shipping and handling (add $1.00 S&H for each additional book). Please make check or money order (please do not send cash) to:

Bob Boardman
P.O. Box 25001
Seattle, WA 98165-1901

Also order by Email (include mailing address) to:
rrboardman@aol.com

By the Author Robert Boardman

C-Rations For The Warrior's Heart

- Foreword by 4-Star General Anthony C. Zinni

- Combat stories from America's principal wars by the author, a recipient of the Silver Star and two Purple Hearts
- Features outstanding warriors from the Marines, Army, Navy and Air Force, many decorated and/or wounded.

- These stories reveal:
  - ✔ that the principle ingredient to victory is the condition of the Inner man.
  - ✔ the struggle for courage, character and victory over fear.

FROM THE FOREWORD

Men discover their true character in the crucible of combat. Few other events in life so test the moral fiber of an Individual. This book is about men who have faced that moment that tried their spirit and how they rose above their fears.

Bob Boardman has given us another labor of love. Like his previous work, Unforgettable Men in Unforgettable Times, It is a book that helps us understand courage. It is a work designed to provide a guide for life's toughest moments with words to comfort, encourage, and counsel.

—Anthony C. Zinni 4-Star General, USMC (Retired)

To order
C-Rations For The Warrior's Heart
send $14.99 (softbound) or $24.95 for hardbound plus $2.95 shipping and handling (add $1.00 S&H for each additional book). Please make check or money order (please do not send cash) to:

Bob Boardman
P.O. Box 25001
Seattle, WA 98165-1901

Also order by Email (include mailing address) to:
rrboardman@aol.com